THE 33-DAY WAR

Gilbert Achcar

with

Michel Warschawski

The 33-Day War

Israel's War on Hezbollah in Lebanon
and its Aftermath

SAQI

London   San Francisco   Beirut

ISBN: 978-0-86356-646-2

A full CIP record for this book is available from the British Library.

Manufactured in Lebanon

SAQI

26 Westbourne Grove, London W2 5RH
825 Page Street, Suite 203, Berkeley, California 94710
Tabet Building, Mneimneh Street, Hamra, Beirut
www.saqibooks.com

Contents

From the Six-Day War to the Thirty-Three-Day War

The Thirty-Three-Day War that Israel waged unsuccessfully against Hezbollah in Lebanon, from July 12 to the dawn of August 14, 2006, has in Arab minds already compensated for the humiliation of the Six-Day War waged from the dawn of June 5 to the evening of June 10, 1967. Conversely, it has set off a major crisis within the Zionist state, where Lebanon confirmed its image as Israel's Vietnam, the image it acquired at the time of the Israeli withdrawal from southern Lebanon in 2000, after eighteen years of occupation.

The war of the summer of 2006 has been classified in various ways, as either the sixth round of the Arab-Israeli war – 1948, 1956, 1967, 1973, 1982, 2006 – or the third Israeli invasion of Lebanon – 1978, 1982, 2006. (Curiously enough, Israel's invasion of southern Lebanon in 1978 as well as the actual war that Israel has been waging against the Palestinian territories since the fall of 2000 are generally not counted among Arab-Israeli wars.)

This series of dates is an eloquent testimony to the gravity of a situation that became an endless tragedy several decades ago. The escalation in the intensity of violence from one war to the other, along with the technological evolution of the armament used on both sides, points to a frightening future. This happens at a time when a new wave of nuclear proliferation is unfolding worldwide, increasing year after year the likelihood that weapons of mass destruction will be used, whether by states or by organizations.

Moreover, of all the hot zones of the world, the Middle East is the one that has generated and continues increasingly to generate the highest amount of violence on a world scale, beyond the zone itself. That is why conflicts in the Middle East attract more attention than those of many other areas: regularly and brutally, they remind the rest of the world of their existence.

This book presents an analysis of the Thirty-Three-Day War in the context of the evolution of Lebanon on whose soil it largely took place, with a focus on its consequences in Lebanon as well as in Israel. It is meant for those who seek a synthetic introduction to this extremely complex problem as well as for those who know the facts already and seek a discussion of their interpretation and of the prospects of this explosive situation.

The authors belong to the two countries that were

directly involved in the war of the summer of 2006, the two enemy states of Israel and Lebanon. Their friendship is more than thirty years old and is all the stronger for transcending the burning border separating their two countries. It is based on their common dedication to the motto of the French Revolution that they learned in school as part of the French education that they share: "Liberty, Equality, Brotherhood" (and Sisterhood). Michel Warschawski wrote Chapter 4, which is devoted to Israel (Marie Stuart translated it from the French); Gilbert Achcar is the author of the rest of the book.

ONE

Lebanon, from its Origins to July 12, 2006

As an "independent" state,[1] Lebanon has always been a site of regional and international conflicts extending far beyond the country itself. In particular, it was a theater of what Malcolm Kerr called "the Arab Cold War"[2] as well as of the global Cold War.

The Precariousness of the Lebanese State

Within its present borders, drawn by the authorities of the French colonial mandate over Syria and Lebanon in 1920, the Lebanese state was built on a precarious religious equilibrium: the enlargement of the borders of the original Lebanese entity created a country with a small

Christian majority, mainly Maronite.[3] France, which prides itself as being the flagship of secularism and republican integration, cut the whole of Greater Syria placed under its tutelage after World War I into denominational (Alawite, Druze) and provincial (Aleppo, Alexandretta, Damascus) states following the worst imperial tradition of "divide and rule." In Lebanon, it set up a political formula based on a sectarian sharing out of powers that was going to last.

The "National Pact" on which independent Lebanon was founded – a 1943 agreement between representatives of the Lebanese dominant classes belonging to the major religious communities – sanctioned the sectarian distribution of positions and seats in the Lebanese state according to a rule that gave a 6–11 majority to Christians. It set up Lebanon on "two negations," as Lebanese editorialist Georges Naccache aptly and famously put it[4]: the Christians renounced French protection, and the Muslims gave up the demand of Greater Syrian unity, for a sovereign Lebanon whose Arab character was vaguely recognized. Fifteen years later, this "pact" was put to a major test for the first time.

In 1958, the first civil conflict in the history of independent Lebanon resulted from the clash between two opposite pressures: on the one hand, the impact of "Nasserism"[5] with its call for the unification of the Arab nation, inaugurated the same year by the union between Egypt and Syria; and, on the other hand, the vehement rejection of this perspective by a segment of the Lebanese population, largely consisting of Christians. Lebanese

President Camille Chamoun supported the Eisenhower Doctrine and the Baghdad Pact, and sought to incorporate the country in the Anglo-American regional strategic system.

This first conflagration, which did not last long, led to the landing in Lebanon, in July 1958, of the Marines sent by U.S. President Dwight Eisenhower. It ended in a compromise that put in power General Fuad Chehab, who ruled the country in a "Bonapartist" fashion, combining authoritarian power based on the military apparatus, arbitration between the various communities, and administrative and social reformism. This compromise exploded under the shock of the June 1967 Arab-Israeli war: although Lebanon was not directly involved in that war, it suffered its consequences in full as it sheltered since 1948 the second-largest number of Palestinian refugees (after Jordan). Radicalization of Palestinians as an outcome of the war, amplified by that of a segment of the Lebanese population, mostly Muslims, disrupted the precarious equilibrium of "Chehabism," prompting another segment, mostly Christians, to throw itself again into Washington's arms.

Meanwhile, social tensions had considerably sharpened in Lebanon. The rapid economic growth of the 1950s and 1960s had disproportionately benefited various regions and communities. Whereas the capital and adjacent regions with a Maronite majority thrived – Beirut became an important transport, trade, and finance hub for the whole of the Arab Middle East – the outlying regions, with a Shiite majority, located all along Lebanon's terrestrial borders, were left outside this dazzling growth.

The differentials among demographic growth rates in the various communities widened, with the poorest bearing the most children, following a well-known sociological trend. In the 1970s, the Shiites became the largest Lebanese community; at the same time, the overpopulation of rural areas triggered an important exodus, which in turn fed the expansion of plebeian periurban zones to the south and east of the capital – to the point that the "Greater Beirut" area alone ended up including one-half of the Lebanese population.

The Civil War, 1975–1990

The combined effect of these structural and political factors led in 1975 to the outbreak of a civil war that was also a regional and international war on Lebanese soil. A year later, after having initially backed the alliance encompassing some Lebanese Muslim groups, all of the Lebanese left-wing forces, and the Palestine Liberation Organization (PLO), the Syrian regime sent its army to rescue the Christian right-wing forces – with Washington's blessing and a green light from the Israelis. Damascus expected to be rewarded by having its interests taken into account in the settlement of the Arab-Israeli conflict.

This Syrian–American entente shattered after one year, however, with a new reversal in positions due to the coming to power of the right-wing Likud in Israel, followed by Egyptian President Anwar al-Sadat's "initiative" of breaking Arab ranks in order to negotiate separately a peace deal with the new Israeli government. Israel then allowed itself to invade part of southern Lebanon in 1978 (an action known as "Operation Litani," named after the river in southern Lebanon beyond which Israel tried to force back the Palestinian armed presence), seeking to create for itself a "security zone" controlled by Lebanese auxiliaries. Having accomplished their mission, the Israeli forces withdrew after a few weeks, giving way to the United Nations Interim Force in Lebanon (UNIFIL), whose "interim" seems unlikely to end soon.

Following the completion in April 1982 of Israel's withdrawal from 1967–occupied Egyptian Sinai, in conformity with the Egyptian–Israeli peace treaty signed in 1979, Menachem Begin's government, with Ariel Sharon at the helm of the defense ministry, believed that the time had come to settle its account once and for all with the PLO. On June 6, 1982, Israel launched a massive military offensive in which the Israeli army invaded Lebanon up to Beirut under the pretext of protecting northern Israel from Palestinian rockets and incursions (the operation was thus named "Peace in Galilee"), even though these clashes had come to a halt several months beforehand. The siege of the Lebanese capital continued for several weeks and led to the evacuation – by sea – of PLO fighters, soon to be followed by the massacre of Palestinian civilians left without protection in the Sabra and Shatila camps under Israeli supervision. After completing its withdrawal from the rest of the country in 1985, Israel occupied southern Lebanon for eighteen years, until the year 2000 – affecting more than one-tenth of the Lebanese territory. The fight against this occupation was the first motivation for the creation of Hezbollah and the main source of the considerable popular legitimacy that it managed to acquire.[6]

The Lebanese civil war, which was interrupted in the fall of 1976 under the aegis of the Syrian–American entente and Saudi sponsorship (Riyadh summit, October 1976), erupted again after this entente broke up. The restoration of the same entente brought the civil war to a conclusion in 1990 following several bloody episodes and a new Saudi mediation (Taif Agreement, October 1989). Indeed, when Iraq invaded Kuwait in August 1990, Syrian dictator Hafez al-Assad joined the coalition led by Washington against Baghdad. This earned him a green light from the United States for an offensive in Lebanon aimed at suppressing the rebellion led by General Michel Aoun. The latter had proclaimed a quixotic "war of liberation" against Syrian troops in 1989, a few months after outgoing President Amine Gemayel handed the power over to him. Aoun found himself completely isolated and was obliged to go into exile in France, from which he returned only after the departure of Syrian troops in 2005.

The 1990 episode brought a lasting end to fifteen years of civil war and allowed the situation in Lebanon to stabilize anew on the basis of the Taif Agreement. The latter provided for a new sectarian distribution of power in favor of Muslims: from then on, parliamentary seats were equally split between Christians and Muslims instead of the 6–11 Christian majority decided in 1943. Moreover, the powers of the Sunni prime minister, henceforth elected by parliament, were considerably increased to the detriment of those of the Maronite president of the republic. This led to the establishment of Rafic Hariri at the center stage of Lebanese politics in the 1990s. A close collaborator of the Saudi ruling family, who allowed him to accumulate a huge personal wealth, Hariri ruled in agreement with the Syrians, as well as their army and *mukhabarat*,[7] at a time when nobody was asking for their immediate departure since the Lebanese state required reconstruction and temporarily needed a "borrowed army."

Washington and Paris Versus Tehran and Damascus

The setup that presided over the end of the Lebanese internecine war broke up again with the second Iraq war. In contrast to his father – but aligning himself, like the latter, behind the position taken by Moscow, the main partner of Baathist Syria outside the Middle East – Bashar al-Assad categorically opposed the U.S. invasion, while strengthening his alliance with Tehran. He thus precipitated a break with both the Americans and the Saudis. It was then that Rafic Hariri came into conflict with pro-Syrian Lebanese President Emile Lahoud, whose mandate Damascus had decided to prorogate in 2004.

The United States – after consolidating its occupation of Iraq following its overthrow of Saddam Hussein's regime, the Syrian regime's rival from within the same Baathist tradition – now turned against Iran, the other state in the region that George W. Bush had designated as part of the "axis of evil" after U.S. forces invaded Afghanistan in the wake of September 11, 2001. In Washington's view, the Iranian regime was, from that point forward, first on the list of enemies to be brought down in order to consolidate U.S. control over Iraq itself as well as to complete the drive for U.S. hegemony over the whole Middle East.

Indeed, it has been Washington's belief that the principal obstacle to its regional domination is a Tehran-led arc of forces that includes Iraqi Iran-allied Shiite forces, the Syrian regime, Lebanese Hezbollah, and Palestinian Hamas. It needed to act against this alliance whose weakest link was apparently Lebanon, where two prime targets could be hit at once: Syrian hegemony over the country and Hezbollah. With this goal in mind, Washington urged the UN Security Council to adopt Resolution 1559 (September 2004), which demanded the withdrawal of Syrian troops from Lebanon and "the disbanding and disarmament of all Lebanese and non-Lebanese militias" – in other words, the disarmament of Hezbollah and of Palestinian refugee camps (where armed organizations allied with Damascus are located).

Resolution 1559 is both a flagrant violation of the UN Charter and a monument to hypocrisy. Adopted against the will of the Lebanese government, which was then pro-

Syrian, it proclaims its attachment to the sovereignty of Lebanon while interfering in its internal affairs in violation of article 2, point 7, of the Charter, which prohibits any intervention "in matters which are essentially within the domestic jurisdiction of any state." Moreover, one would have to be extraordinarily naive to believe for a single instant that the permanent members of the Security Council are attached to the sovereignty of any state other than their own. Resolution 1559 – and the fact that it was adopted in 2004, not before, amply demonstrates this – was quite obviously consistent with U.S. action against Iran and its allies, when it became the highest priority, after Afghanistan and Iraq, as the third stage in the imperial offensive launched by the Bush administration in the "Greater Middle East."

On this issue, France – contrary to its attitude on the issue of Iraq, but in conformity with the attitude that presided over its zealous participation in the Afghan expedition – collaborated fully and actively with the United States. In the Iraqi affair, contradictory interests with regard to each country's oil designs motivated Paris and Washington. When Israel decided in the 1960s to replace France with the United States as its regular supplier of weapons, Paris changed its Middle East policy. Charles de Gaulle's criticism of Israel after the June 1967 war signaled this change – a criticism made all the more dramatic by its anti-Semitic undertone. Since then, French policy in this part of the world – chiefly inspired by the interests of oil firms and arms makers, as well as of aeronautics and construction –

sought above all to penetrate those areas from which U.S. interests were barred. Paris naturally became the privileged Western partner of Moscow's allies.

This is how, in the 1970s, Saddam Hussein's Iraq became France's privileged commercial and political partner in the Middle East – to the point that Paris, during the following decade, took planes (of the "Super-Etendard" type) out of the air fleet of its own armed forces and "lent" them to Iraq in its war against Iran. This privileged collaboration continued in spite of Paris's participation in the coalition led by Washington against Baghdad in the 1991 Gulf War. For all that, Saddam Hussein did not cease granting market and oil concessions to French firms, as well as Russian firms. He thus strengthened these two states' motivation to work for lifting the embargo imposed on Iraq, as the indispensable condition for implementing the concessions they were granted.

The same motivation accounts for why Paris and Moscow embraced a negative attitude toward the second war waged by Washington and London against Baghdad. When the Anglo-American coalition finally occupied Iraq from March 2003 on, an occupation that led to the cancellation of the concessions previously granted to French interests, France gave priority to its other major commercial partner in the region – namely, the Saudi kingdom.[8] The latter, however, in contrast to Saddam Hussein's regime, is the oldest and most important Arab ally of the United States. In Lebanon this resulted, in 2004, in a "competitive convergence" of interests between Paris and Washington, as the "great friendship" between Jacques Chirac and Rafic Hariri (whose relationship has always been highly "rewarding") jibed quite naturally with Paris's assiduous courting of the Saudis. UN Security Council Resolution 1559 was the first fruit of this convergence.

Lebanon After the Departure of Syrian Troops

The withdrawal of Syrian troops occurred in 2005, but not thanks to Resolution 1559, which met with a flat refusal from both Syria and the then pro-Syrian government in Beirut. In actuality, the Syrian withdrawal was precipitated by the impressive mass mobilization that followed the assassination of Rafic Hariri on February 14, 2005, creating in Lebanon an untenable situation for Damascus.

At the same time, new political and sectarian tensions appeared in the country after years of lull, but in an unprecedented form. In particular, they manifested as two gigantic and opposite demonstrations in March 2005. On one side of the coin was the March 8 demonstration, which regrouped most of the Shiite forces (Hezbollah and Amal)[9] as well as pro-Syrian minority forces belonging to the other communities. On the opposite side was the March 14 counterdemonstration called for by an alliance regrouping the majority forces within the Maronite, Sunni, and Druze communities, now led by Hariri Jr. The country was clearly divided into two roughly equal camps. The Saudi kingdom feared a test of strength that risked turning sour and aggravating a regional destabilization that could serve Iran. It advocated calming things down.

The tension diminished markedly with the May–June 2005 parliamentary elections, held after the departure of Syrian troops: a grand coalition brought together the anti-Syrian alliance (designated from then on by the date of its gigantic demonstration on March 14) and the bloc consisting of Shiite forces, Hezbollah, and Amal. The only forces excluded from this understanding were the non-Shiite pro-Syrian groups and General Aoun, despite the fact that his supporters had played a fundamental role in the anti-Syrian mobilization, the March 14 demonstration included. Aoun energetically protested against the decision to organize the elections according to the Syrian-inspired electoral law promulgated in 2000 – a law that aimed notably at minimizing the representation of the "Aounist" movement then held to command a large majority among Maronites and considered by Damascus to be its most dangerous Lebanese enemy.

The March 14 alliance had chosen to favor the Maronite rivals of Michel Aoun, whose political ambitions and anticorruption crusade, coupled with his vehement denunciation of Rafic Hariri when the latter was in power in close collaboration with Damascus, worried both the Hariri group and its allies – the Druze leader Walid Jumblatt in particular. In order to isolate Aoun, the March 14 coalition had sanctioned the electoral law imposed by Syria and cut a deal with the two main Lebanese allies of Damascus – namely, the two Shiite movements. For revenge, Aoun, who until then had consistently expressed an anti-Syrian stance and had boasted about his personal contribution to the drafting of Resolution 1559, started cozying up with pro-Syrian minority Christian forces and stood in opposition to the new parliamentary and governmental majority. Those were only the premises of his major turnabout after the elections.

Indeed, a few months later, to widespread surprise, Michel Aoun joined the whole spectrum of pro-Syrian forces, including the Shiite forces, opposing any action seeking to force the resignation of President Lahoud, whose mandate had been prorogated by Damascus. Aoun explained that, since the Syrian army was gone, there was no longer any contention between himself and Damascus, and thus he was in favor of friendly relations with the Syrian neighbor. On February 6, 2006, he signed a platform of political understanding with Hezbollah, which defined a perspective for the settlement of the issue of the latter's armament.[10] This agreement sealed an Aoun–Hezbollah alliance that has become a major factor in Lebanese politics.

Of course the alliance itself is a marriage of convenience based on two political calculations. The calculation of Michel Aoun – who hopes to obtain the Lebanese presidency and to establish a new Bonapartist regime more or less inspired by the Chehabist precedent – is that his alliance with the Shiites, the largest community, in addition to his own popularity among the Maronites constitute a winning combination for the achievement of his ambition.

His opposition to forcing Lahoud's resignation flows naturally from the fact that he has no chance to succeed him with the parliamentary majority that resulted from the 2005 elections – inasmuch as the president of the republic is elected by parliament in Lebanon. Aoun demands that a new electoral law be promulgated – a demand that is included in his agreement with Hezbollah – and that new parliamentary elections be held prior to the election of a new president.

The calculation of Hezbollah, faced with the increasing pressure of a governmental majority relaying U.S. and French pressure for its disarmament in the name of Resolution 1559, is, of course, to thwart this pressure and hold the majority in check by means of the alliance with Aoun. This alliance prevents the Shiite forces from being isolated in a confrontation against an anti-Syrian and anti-Iranian bloc commanding a majority in all other communities. It also emboldens the minority forces opposed to the March 14 coalition in these other communities. The political fault line thus now runs through the Maronite community, the second-largest after the Shiites, where Aoun stands opposed to the allies of Hariri Jr. and Washington – including the "Lebanese Forces" of Samir Geagea, the Lebanese warlord most implicated personally in massacres perpetrated during the civil war.

For its part, the March 14 coalition tried, without much conviction, to promote the emergence of a Shiite force within its ranks, while attempting more actively to foster the differences between Hezbollah and Amal. These efforts achieved only minimal results, due to the strength of Amal's ties with Damascus and its fear of being marginalized by its much more popular Shiite rival following a rift with it.

Israel's Twin Offensives

The course of events in Lebanon became a source of great frustration for Washington in the wake of the mobilizations and tensions that followed Rafic Hariri's assassination. The Bush administration had hoped that its allies, emboldened by the impressive mobilization of their supporters and by the withdrawal of the Syrian army, would come to terms with the task of disarming Hezbollah. It was soon obvious, however, that the real balance of forces in Lebanon, once free from the troops of Damascus, was not such as to allow Washington's Lebanese allies to risk a test of strength with the Shiite party. To this end, the Lebanese army constituted, and still constitutes, an instrument of little reliability. Any attempt at using it against Hezbollah could lead to its explosion along the lines of what occurred in the spring of 1976 in the first phase of the fifteen-year civil war. The part of UN Resolution 1559 dealing with Hezbollah's disarmament seemed postponed indefinitely.

A conclusion imposed itself: what had become necessary was an intervention from an external power in order to change the balance of forces in Lebanon and, through the same means, to create conditions favorable to decisive action by Washington's Lebanese allies against Hezbollah.

The United States was bogged down in the Iraqi quagmire and France did not have the means, so the task of changing the deal in Lebanon fell to Israel – a new opportunity for the Zionist state to prove its usefulness to Washington's regional designs while defending its own interests. Indeed, ever since its withdrawal of troops from southern Lebanon in 2000, Israel was awaiting an opportunity not only to take revenge against Lebanon's Shiites and Hezbollah but also to restore its deterrent credibility, which had been gravely undermined by the Lebanese episode – at least with regard to popular resistances.

At that point, Washington suffered a second regional setback in its confrontation with Tehran: in January 2006, the Palestinian Hamas won the parliamentary elections in the West Bank and Gaza. The Bush administration reacted immediately in full symbiosis with its Israeli ally, mobilizing its Western allies and exhorting them to ostracize the new Palestinian government and cut off its funding. At the same time, it urged its Palestinian partners, starting with Palestinian Authority President Mahmoud Abbas, not to imitate its Lebanese allies – in other words, not to set up a coalition with Hamas in the name of whichever supreme national interest.

Under the increasing effect of the strangulation to which the Palestinians were submitted, it did not take much time before tensions rose in their midst, fueled by Washington's closest allies among them. The resentment of the Palestinian population, however, like that of Arab public opinion, was directed chiefly against the stranglers rather than against those who had obtained a majority through democratic elections. Israel's increasing exactions against the Palestinian territories incited their population to wish more and more avidly for an implementation of national unity against its traditional oppressor. This aspiration found a decisive momentum in the conclusion, in May, of an agreement over a common national political platform between Palestinian prisoners held in Israel and belonging to almost all Palestinian political currents, from Fatah to Hamas (with the exception of Islamic Jihad).

On June 25, 2006, Palestinian fighters from Gaza abducted an Israeli soldier in reaction to the repeated abduction of Palestinians by the Israeli army – two of them on the very day before – with a view toward using him as a bargaining tool to obtain the liberation of Palestinian prisoners. Then, on June 28, Israel launched its murderous offensive against Gaza, cynically named "Summer Rains." It was presented as a response to the abduction of the Israeli soldier, although it took place a full three days later. Another event was thus overshadowed: on June 27 – that is, on the very eve of the Israeli offensive – Mahmoud Abbas and the leaders of Hamas announced their agreement over an amended version of "the prisoners' document" and the forthcoming establishment of a Palestinian national unity government.

The Israeli offensive launched on June 28, 2006, thus aimed quite obviously at dealing Hamas a heavy blow and enjoining Mahmoud Abbas not to cooperate with the Islamic fundamentalist organization. It sought to achieve that goal by taking the Palestinian population hostage in ways even more oppressive than those employed since the January elections. Moreover, one of the first measures of the offensive was to abduct some twenty Palestinian parliamentary members of Hamas in order to deprive the organization of its parliamentary majority. Israel called on Abbas to take advantage of the situation – which he refrained from doing, as he knew how unpopular such a move would be.

It was in this general context that on July 12, a few days after the onslaught on Gaza had started, Lebanon also came under attack. The two onslaughts had twin goals: in both cases, the objective was to deal a heavy blow to a foe of Israel and Washington and to prompt Washington's local allies to settle their accounts with this foe.

TWO

Hezbollah, from its Origins to July 12, 2006

By the end of the 1960s, the demographic boom of the Shiite community against a background of economic poverty and the rural exodus toward Beirut's plebeian belt constituted a Shiite proletariat, underclass, and poor peasantry – in other words, the perfect constituency for forces embodying social and political radicalization.

From One Radicalization to Another

Radicalization was there indeed: the 1960s had already witnessed a gradual radicalization of Arab nationalism, to the point that some sectors of this political current even switched to Marxism. The June 1967 war then accentuated the global groundswell that was sparked primarily by Vietnamese resistance to U.S. aggression and culminated in 1968, sweeping through many parts of the world, before it subsided at the end of the 1970s with the general crisis affecting global capitalism and the beginning of the agony of the "communist" states.

The post-1967 radicalization found expression in Lebanon in the spectacular growth of left-wing and radical left forces – the Lebanese Communist Party (LCP) in particular – among Shiites above all, whether in poor rural areas or in Beirut's plebeian belt. The traditional leaderships that used to dominate the Shiite community – mostly quasi-feudal large landowners that had converted to electoral feudalism and capitalized on their influence over the community to get lucrative positions in the Lebanese state – lost ground inexorably. The Shiite bourgeoisie, like its counterparts among other communities, worried about the rise of the radical left.

It was chiefly in an effort to face this situation that, in 1974, a Shiite religious dignitary, Musa al-Sadr, and an enlightened member of the Shiite "political class," the MP Hussein el-Husseini, founded the Movement of the Deprived (*mahrumeen*), which in turn set up an armed wing known as Amal ("Hope") – the Arab acronym of Lebanese Resistance Battalions. The Movement of the Deprived competed against the Lebanese left on its own social ground not only by organizing all kinds of services – thanks to the important financial means that were at its disposal from the start – but also by resorting to a populist discourse that outbid the left. Thus, addressing an impressive mass rally organized by his movement in its early period, the charismatic Musa al-Sadr denounced the existence of thousands of vacant apartments in Beirut at a time when the masses of "deprived" Shiites were crammed together in unsanitary conditions within the capital's periphery.

Musa al-Sadr's movement set itself up as the mouthpiece of the Shiite community, demanding a larger share for its representatives in the institutions according to the tradition of the sectarian political system existing in Lebanon. With regard to the Lebanese left and the Palestinians, its attitude fluctuated over time between amicable competition (and even collaboration with Yasir Arafat's Fatah at the beginning) and virulent opposition. During the long Lebanese civil war, Amal clashed several times with either Lebanese Communists or Nasserites as well as with Palestinian organizations. Its links with the Syrian regime became a main aspect of its political identity, especially after its founder Musa al-Sadr "disappeared" during a visit to Libya in 1978.

A major event took place the following year, signaling a shift in the political history of the Middle East: the "Islamic Revolution" headed by Ayatollah Ruhollah Khomeini overthrew the Shah of Iran and established in Tehran a theocratic regime fiercely opposed to the United States, which was designated as the "Great Satan." During the preceding quarter of a century, Islamic fundamentalism had been the favorite ideological weapon of reactionary forces backed by Washington in the Muslim world. These were led by the Saudi kingdom, with its fiercely rigorist and obscurantist regime based on Wahhabism, the crudest version of Islamic fundamentalism. What appeared here quite suddenly was a highly impressive manifestation of another brand of Islamic fundamentalism, one that set itself up as the bearer of radical opposition to the West.

Islamic fundamentalism of the old type, allied with the West in the fight against communism, continued to be employed by Washington and its Saudi and Pakistani friends in the war against the Soviet occupation of Afghanistan in the 1980s. They justified their carry-over of the same policy on the grounds that Iranian Shiite Islam was very different from the Muslim world's majority Sunni Islam, held to be resistant to the anti-Americanism advocated by Tehran's new regime. However, the end of the Soviet Union and the turnaround of major sections of Sunni fundamentalism, following the U.S. intervention against Iraq and the deployment of U.S. troops in the Arabian Peninsula, increasingly compromised the United States' irritation with Islamic fundamentalism, especially after September 11, 2001. But Washington is an apprentice-sorcerer that is obviously incapable of finishing its apprenticeship – and these foregoing events did not prevent it from once again allying, despite all, with the Afghan fundamentalist forces of the Northern Alliance in order to overthrow the Taliban and rule Afghanistan. Nor did they prevent it from collaborating with Iraqi fundamentalists, whether Shiite or Sunni, in the management of occupied Iraq.

The Growth and Mutation of Hezbollah

Hezbollah, "the Party of God," was born at the junction of the shockwave of the Iranian revolution and the situation created in Lebanon three years later by the 1982 Israeli invasion. The "Islamic Revolution" gave a huge impulsion to anti-Western Islamic fundamentalism in the whole of the Muslim world, helping it to occupy the ground left vacant by the failure of more or less progressive brands of nationalism and the shortcoming of the radical left: the ground on which the struggle against Western domination and its local despotic allies has been waged.

It was thus Hezbollah that managed to channel into its ranks the subsequent wave of radicalization among Lebanese Shiites, who were naturally the most receptive by virtue of their sectarian affinity to the influence of the Iranian revolution. The 1982 Israeli invasion, coming on top of the already considerable impact of the Iranian revolution, accelerated a radicalization within Amal and the emergence of an "Islamic" splinter group holding the banner of Khomeinism, tolerated until then within the ranks of the movement. Officially proclaimed in 1985 under this name, Hezbollah built itself (since its inception in 1982) with direct aid – ideological, as well as political, military, and financial – from Tehran. It set itself the task of taking the lead in the struggle against the Israeli occupation, waging at the same time a political and ideological struggle for hegemony over Lebanese Shiites.

Hezbollah thus counterposed its Khomeinist radicalism

shaped in the mold of Iranian Islamic fundamentalism –
adherence to the model of the "Islamic Republic" and to the
theocratic principle of *velayat-e faqih* ("guardianship of the
theologian-jurist"), as well as allegiance to the "Supreme
Leader" Khomeini, and to his radical hostility toward
Israel,[1] Western domination, and its Lebanese brokers
– against what it perceived to be Amal's compromise of
principle in the rotten deals of Lebanese politics. Funds
granted to Hezbollah by Iran quickly became greater
than those Amal had at its disposal in the absence of a
sponsor as important and rich as Tehran. Used smartly,
with a remarkable immunity to corruption compared with
other Lebanese forces, Iranian funds were employed by
Hezbollah to set up a network of social services competing
with Amal's and surpassing it, allowing the party to acquire
an important mass base within the Shiite community.[2] In
return, the growth of its community base increased its
financial means, particularly through the religious taxation
that it imposes on its supporters.

In an early phase of its establishment, Hezbollah waged
a fierce fight against its rivals among Shiites. One force it
considered a rival to be brushed aside was the Lebanese
Communist Party, which had an important Shiite
constituency and, moreover, had started the anti-Israeli
resistance in 1982 – an initiative that put it in a position
to capture (to the detriment of Amal) the radicalization
potential created by the invasion. With the Communists,
the fight was not only ideological: Hezbollah has been
strongly suspected of bearing responsibility for the

assassination of several Communist activists, including some of the foremost Shiite Communist personalities, in the years following its official proclamation in 1985. In 1987, bloody clashes opposed Hezbollah to Syrian troops and, in the following year, to Amal itself.

Hezbollah sought to monopolize the prestige of the resistance to the occupier to the benefit of the "Islamic Resistance" that it constituted as a rival force to the "National Resistance" of the secular political forces. To this end, to be sure, it set itself apart through its dedication to the fight and its aptitude for offering "martyrs" to the cause, as well as through the training and military means that it got from Iran. But it also sought to impose by force its monopoly on the armed struggle in regions under its control in the resistance area in southern Lebanon. Amal did the same in the rural areas under its own control, thus contributing to hindering the Communists' resistance fight.[3] In the year 2000, when Israel decided under compulsion to evacuate the last portion of the Lebanese territory that it occupied in 1982, Hezbollah claimed the whole prestige of this victory for its own – deservingly so indeed, but its claim also obscured the far-from negligible role of other resistance currents, whether secular or left wing.

After an initial period characterized by merciless competition, Hezbollah established a pattern of coexistence with the other organizations rooted in the Shiite community. Tehran's mediation sealed its alliance with Amal as well as with the Syrian regime. Over the years, the party underwent a mutation whereby its status as a mass party gradually overtook its role as an armed resistance organization. This mutation was accelerated by changes that took place in Iran following the demise of Ayatollah Khomeini in 1989: the very "pragmatic" Ali Akbar Hashemi Rafsanjani became president while Ayatollah Ali Khamenei got promoted to the rank of "Supreme Leader." It was also accelerated, of course, by the turn in the Lebanese political situation represented by the Taif Agreement of the same year – 1989 – and the end of the civil war the year after.

Hezbollah then entered the political and institutional arena in the pacified Lebanon of the 1990s, becoming one of the major forces on the Lebanese political scene. This outcome was facilitated by the fact that, very early on, the party had qualified its foundational inspiration by acknowledging the unsuitability of the "Islamic Republic" program for multi-religious Lebanon, contenting itself with building its hegemony over the Shiite community and with using this position of strength to exert an influence over Lebanon's political evolution.

Khomeinism Adapted to Lebanese Reality

Since its very first programmatic proclamation, the 1985 "Letter to the Oppressed" (*mustazafeen*),[4] Hezbollah asserted that the prospect of an Islamic state on the Iranian model is impossible in Lebanon unless the sectarian composition of the country was changed by force, or a secession provoked. In its effort to reassure the Lebanese Christians, the new party – while it invited the Christians to convert to Islam and all the Lebanese to opt for an Islamic government – made it clear that it did not intend to impose this option by force. In return, it rejected the Christians' "sectarian privileges," thus subscribing to the ideology that is dominant in Lebanon and following which power is seen through the prism of sectarian inequalities instead of social inequalities. The *mustazafeen* were thus considered to be at a disadvantage as a religious community and not as subaltern social layers.

With its increasing insertion into the Lebanese social fabric, Hezbollah exchanged the fundamentalist program of its foundational Khomeinist inspiration for adherence of a special kind to the Ottoman-inspired principle upon which Lebanese institutions are based: the "millet" system. According to this system, each religious community enjoys a certain degree of autonomy in the organization of its religious affairs and civil code – citizenship existing only through the intermediation of the religious community.[5] The party subscribes fully to this principle, which it extends far beyond personal status issues. Indeed, it practices a far more extensive autonomy in the areas under its control – a political, social, cultural, and even partly judicial autonomy – by means of its political–religious organization, its network of social services, and its educational and financial institutions.

In that sense, it is not, properly speaking, a "counter-society" that Hezbollah is managing: this analytical concept, first developed with regard to what the French Communist Party used to be, was applied to Hezbollah by Lebanese sociologist Waddah Charara.[6] It refers to a type of organization that aspires to be the embryo of a social system bound to replace the existing capitalist society. The communal organization of Hezbollah is not – and could not reasonably be – intended for extension to the whole of Lebanese society. It contents itself, therefore, with its "natural" sphere of implementation – namely, its sectarian constituency – in coexistence with the political and religious organizations of the other communities and the state apparatus instead of being counterposed to them.

There is indeed a "Hezbollah state," as implied by Charara's title – or, more accurately, a substate within the Lebanese state – but this is not uncommon in Lebanon, which has inexorably evolved, ever since the "Chehabist" project failed, into a federation of communities according to a new, amplified version of the Ottoman system. A peculiarity of the Lebanese formula is that it allows for the existence within the same religious community of subcommunities that are based on political allegiances and have various substatal elements at their disposal. In that sense, Lebanon is still living under the warlords system that prevailed after the outbreak of the civil war in 1975.

This explains why Hezbollah does not have much trouble adhering to the Taif compromise of 1989 – 1990, whether with regard to balancing the sectarian sharing-out of power in Lebanon or to "abolishing political sectarianism."

This second goal implies the suppression of any sectarian sharing-out of seats and posts within Lebanese institutions, a reform that would allow for the free expression of the real balance of forces between the political–sectarian currents. As the major force within the largest Lebanese community, Hezbollah stands only to win from such a suppression, which should not be confused with secularization – that is, with the establishment of a civil code for personal status that would transcend all communities, and the strict separation of religion and state – inasmuch as secularization is in fundamental contradiction with Hezbollah's original Islamic fundamentalism. The latter ideology is a source of reactionary attitudes regarding gender relations and questions of private and public morality, even though the party's attitude toward women is less backward than that of the principal bastions of Sunni Islamic fundamentalism, in the same sense that Iran is much less backward than the Saudi kingdom.

Hezbollah's originality with regard to its Iranian model finds expression in the party's relationship with Tehran. The Islamic Republic of Iran remains the supreme reference of the party, which submits its own programmatic orientations to doctrinal approval by the Iranian "Supreme Leader." Yet, for all that, the party is not simply an outlet of the Iranian regime, under direct control from Tehran. It enjoys a real autonomy that Iran grants all the more willingly given that it is a highly important ally – one that could well distance itself from the Islamic Republic, if ever Tehran's guardianship became too heavy, even if doing so led to a significant decrease in its resources. This, however, is only a remote possibility, and the Lebanese party remains the most prestigious member of the regional family of Khomeinism to which the Supreme Council for the Islamic Revolution in Iraq (SCIRI) belongs as well – a family that constitutes the hardcore component of the more informal regional alliance that binds Iran with Sunni Palestinian Hamas and the "secular" Syrian regime.

From the foregoing, as well as from the history of the organization itself, it follows that Hezbollah's allegiance to Tehran and its alliance with Damascus are on altogether different levels, even though Syria is the necessary way through for Iranian armaments sent to Hezbollah and, for this reason, holds an important means of pressure over the Lebanese organization. Besides, and at any rate, Hezbollah is less dependent on support from Tehran and Damascus than Israel is on Washington's support, if only because it is easier for an organization than for a structurally dependent state to do without the external support that it usually gets, by reducing its expenditure if need be. In this respect, the United States' and Israel's criticism of Hezbollah for its allegiance to Iran is indeed an expression of the infinite arrogance that the two countries share.[7]

Resistance and Charity

Hezbollah's mutation in the 1990s was facilitated by the

accession to the head of the party – to the post of "general secretary" – of Hassan Nasrallah, a very pragmatic leader. This occurred in the aftermath of Israel's assassination of his predecessor in 1992. Hezbollah regularly took part in parliamentary elections from that year on – the year of the first elections in Lebanon since 1972 – and has had several MPs ever since. It became by far the most popular force in the Shiite community, a popularity due largely to the social services organized by the party and the fight it waged against Israeli occupation of southern Lebanon. Israel's withdrawal in 2000 constituted a major event in the already long history of the Arab-Israeli conflict: for the first time since the birth of the Israeli state, its armed forces evacuated a conquered territory unconditionally, under compulsion from a guerilla struggle and not due to international pressure.

Hezbollah's fight was the source of a double legitimation for the party, not only politically but also with regard to its armament, which it kept in the name of resistance against the occupier at a time, after 1990, when the other Lebanese political forces were submitting themselves to more or less effective disarmament, in accordance with the Taif Agreement. After 2000, Hezbollah entertained this legitimation by pointing to issues relating to the Israeli-Lebanese conflict that remain unresolved – namely, the area designated as Shebaa Farms and Kfarshuba Heights, occupied since 1967;[8] the Lebanese prisoners detained by Israel; and, above all, Israel's propensity for encroaching on Lebanese sovereignty by land, air, and sea, thus keeping the country under the threat of a new invasion.

This last fact is actually the major argument legitimizing Hezbollah's armament, whether for its own defense or that of the Shiite areas of southern Lebanon that were repeatedly attacked by Israel, or as a deterrent against a new Israeli occupation of Lebanese territory. The party's prestige was enhanced by the prisoner deal that took place in January 2004, through which Hezbollah obtained from Israel the liberation of 435 Lebanese and Palestinian prisoners, as well as the mortal remains of close to 60 militants, in exchange for 1 Israeli hostage and the bodies of 3 soldiers. This operation confirmed the party's conviction that the only way to obtain the liberation of the Lebanese prisoners still held in Israel – among them Samir Kuntar, detained since 1979 as a result of his participation in a commando attack by the Palestine Liberation Front – is to exchange them for Israeli hostages.

Until the departure of Israeli troops from Lebanon, Hezbollah had reservations about participating in government, preferring to avoid the risk of being associated against its will in decisions that could have been in contradiction with its ideology or political orientations – and this so as not to enter into conflict with Damascus, the real seat of power.[9] The withdrawal of Syrian troops completed in 2005 before the parliamentary elections of the same year changed the situation: the Lebanese government became again an autonomous source of decisions affecting the country's future. Hezbollah decided therefore to be represented in government by two ministers, in the wake of its electoral agreement with the forces of the anti-Syrian March 14 alliance.

Nonetheless, the forces holding a majority in parliament as well as in the government headed by Fouad Siniora – a member of the "Hariri group" in the political and entrepreneurial sense – started demanding Hezbollah's disarmament, invoking UN Security Council Resolution 1559 under Washington's pressure. While it maintained its participation in government, Hezbollah was driven to side with the opposition – a situation that was sanctioned by the alliance sealed between Hezbollah and Michel Aoun in February 2006.

The very same circumstances drove the party – in collaboration with the rest of the opposition, including the Communists but also General Aoun's movement and other groups that it would occur to nobody to regard as left-wing forces – to oppose some particularly unpopular neoliberal measures that the Siniora government tried to implement. This did not happen without some hesitation, moreover: of the two Hezbollah ministers in the Siniora government, one, the minister of Labor, participated in this capacity in the Higher Council for Privatization, whereas the other, the minister of Electricity, had some misgivings about the project of privatizing the sector under his responsibility. The opportunity for making use of a popular cause against the governmental majority, the pressure of the Communist allies, and, above all, the fact that the privatization of electricity would be detrimental chiefly to Hezbollah's plebeian base finally convinced the minister to abandon the project.

The fact is that nothing in Hezbollah's programmatic orientation, which is particularly vague on these issues, opposes capitalism – even its neoliberal version. The party did not set itself up as an opposition force to Rafic Hariri's neoliberal orientations when the latter was standing at the helm of the Lebanese government, nor do such orientations hamper its alliances with anybody. It was thanks to its electoral agreement with Hezbollah that the March 14 coalition, led by Hariri Jr., was able to secure a comfortable majority in the Lebanese parliament. However, the plebeian composition of the party's social base is a source of pressure for a policy of opposition to the most unpopular social and economic reforms. The diversity of the social layers that are represented within Hezbollah's ranks and at the party's periphery can even cause divides on such issues – similar to the divides that, within the Iranian regime, still pit populist currents against traditionally capitalist currents.

In the social–economic field, social justice in the party's understanding does not go beyond the redistribution by way of taxation that the Islamic Sharia provides for. Hezbollah recycles the funds that it takes from its social environment, as well as those it gets from Iran, into a policy of help to needy people, which – far from constituting them as a force for social change – contributes to maintaining their resignation to their fate. That is precisely what a recent editorial in *al-Akhbar*, the Lebanese daily closest to Hezbollah, explained very clearly:

Since the return of civil peace and the beginning of the reconstruction of the state, [the] elites acceded to power and enjoyed sweet life, while the poorest sectors of the population continued to fight and sacrifice themselves for the liberation of occupied southern Lebanon. By insisting on the priority of the battle for liberation with regard to other political and social domestic battles, and by mobilizing for this battle the forces of its numerous masses, deprived in their majority, Hezbollah contributed to maintaining social "peace" in Lebanon.

In other circumstances, the unjust neoliberal policies that were adopted in the phase of reconstruction [during the 1990s] should have provoked violent social insurrections. Through its social, educative and charity institutions and associations, the party has succeeded in weaving a social safety net for large sectors of the Lebanese population, in the absence of any social policy of the state. The already mentioned elites should have thanked Hezbollah, but instead, they have continued to attack it.[10]

The Hostage Taking of July 12, 2006

Keen on defending the Lebanese legitimacy of its armament, Hezbollah raised its voice over two issues in particular: the

Shebaa Farms and the Lebanese prisoners held in Israel.[11] In a speech delivered on April 24, 2006, at a ceremony marking the twenty-eighth anniversary of Samir Kuntar's detention, Hassan Nasrallah pledged publicly to act for the liberation of the detainee, announcing that it would take place "very very very soon" and hinting at an imminent "resistance action" toward this end. Hezbollah's chief was still more precise, as he confirmed that Israel was already expecting an attempt to abduct Israeli soldiers: "During the whole of last month and until this day, the Israeli state of alert along the whole Lebanese border with occupied Palestine has remained at its highest level. During this period, official and international contacts were taken with us to inform us that the reason for the Israeli state of alert is their fear that you may abduct or apprehend an Israeli soldier."[12] Hezbollah does appear to have started preparing in March for the abduction of Israeli soldiers that finally took place on July 12, 2006; Nasrallah himself declared, on the day of the operation, that it had been in preparation for five months. In July, regional circumstances had added a supplementary political value to the operation: indeed, since June 28, Israel had launched its military operation against the Palestinian territory of Gaza, seizing the abduction of one of its soldiers as a pretext. In light of the scope and violence of the Israeli onslaught on Gaza, a brutal Israeli reaction against Lebanon was to be expected if Israeli soldiers were to be abducted by Hezbollah a few days after the Palestinian precedent.

Hezbollah's leadership believed, however, that it would

not be that serious. In a long interview published on April 27, 2006, in the Lebanese daily *as-Safir*, Nasrallah explained that, since the northern region is Israel's most important one and since the Israeli leaders know that Hezbollah holds the means to bomb it if Israel aggresses against Lebanon, they will "count to one thousand" before launching a new aggression. This was a major error in calculation – a clear underestimation of Israel's determination not to tolerate whatever form of regional deterrence would hamper its freedom of movement. Hezbollah's chief honestly recognized his error later on, in the interview he gave to the Lebanese New TV channel on August 27, 2006:

> We had not foreseen, not even to one-hundredth, that the hostage taking would lead to a war of that scope. *Why?* Because of several decades of experience, and because we know how the Israeli acts, it was not possible that a reaction to a hostage taking reaches such proportions, especially in the middle of the tourist season. In the history of wars, it never happened that a state launches a war against another state for a few apprehended soldiers and a few others killed. Now if you ask me [what we would have done] if I had known that this abduction would lead to a war of such a dimension with one per cent probability, well, we would certainly not have done it, for

human, moral, military, social, security and political reasons.[13]

In the course of the same interview, Nasrallah emphasized quite rightly that the Israeli aggression against Lebanon was premeditated. He referred to investigations done after the war, especially in the United States,[14] indicating that the plan for the offensive had been devised by Israel in concert with Washington and that the July 12 operation was merely the pretext allowing Israel to carry it out. But Hezbollah's leader minimized the importance of the pretext that his organization's action had provided, asserting that the Israeli services themselves would have created one if needed, at whatever time Israel deemed to be the most appropriate to launch its offensive – namely, the fall of 2006, according to Nasrallah.

What remains beyond question, at any rate, is that the Israeli offensive was premeditated. Israeli officials themselves have clearly hinted at the fact that it was planned long ago, and that they were waiting for a politically appropriate opportunity to launch it. Indeed, as Prime Minister Ehud Olmert candidly told the London *Times*:

> I heard there were some voices that said that Israel should have attacked Lebanon before, during the last five years since we pulled out because of what we have seen created [there] – a big infrastructure created for Hezbollah.
>
> I have to be very honest with you. I was

only part of the time a member of the cabinet.
But just for the sake of argument, could you
imagine [Ariel] Sharon initiating an attack on
Lebanon any time in these five years that could
have won the slightest possible support from
anyone?

... But let's be honest, had he done
anything at that time, particularly without such
a provocation that I have encountered this
time, what would have been the reaction of
the world? What would have been the reaction
even of the public opinion of Israel?[15]

With the same frankness, Brigadier General Yossi
Kuperwasser, until recently head of the research division of
Military Intelligence, replied to a journalist from *Haaretz*
who asked him whether anyone during the preceding years
had advocated a preventive strike against Hezbollah: "No,
no one said that, because it's clear that it's impossible to do
it. To do something like that you have to adopt an approach
for which the Americans were unable to mobilize world
support. An approach based on a preventive strike. When
the United States went into Iraq to carry out a preventive
move, it did not succeed in obtaining international backing.
So do you want Israel to do that? Let's be serious."[16]

Statements by nonofficial personalities were even more
direct, as when Ron Pundak, director general of the Peres
Center for Peace and a former Israeli negotiator with the
Palestinians, told the *New York Times:* "Hezbollah gave

them a wonderful option to do something the army was already prepared to do, with a well-constructed operational plan on the shelf."[17] These statements, and many others, confirm without beating around the bush that the 2006 aggression against Lebanon had been designed long in advance, but was waiting for political conditions that could secure for Israel resolute international support – including support by the United States free from any political embarrassment as well as support expressed through Israeli public opinion. From this angle, the hostage taking of July 12, although it can certainly be considered legitimate resistance action, was particularly ill conceived and wrongly timed. It allowed the Israeli government to launch, without any restraint, an offensive of unprecedented violence and destructive fury, with the explicit or tacit support of all Western powers – even though the extended bombing earned Israel a few derisory reproaches expressed in the form of friendly advice by some European governments.

Washington and its Arab allies were able to hold Hezbollah responsible for the outbreak of hostilities, and even to accuse it of having deliberately triggered them on Tehran's order. The endorsement that the United States and its European allies gave to the new Israeli aggression, which was presented as Israel's exercise of its right to "legitimate defense," was less inhibited than any previous endorsement of an Israeli aggression against Lebanon. But although it had given Israel a good pretext through an error in calculation, Hezbollah succeeded in containing the Israeli aggression to a remarkable degree and in reversing the situation to its advantage. At the end of the day, Israel's error in calculation proved far more serious than Hezbollah's error.

THREE

The Thirty-Three-Day War and its Consequences in Lebanon

In order to appreciate what was at stake in the Thirty-Three-Day War, to draw its balance sheet, and to understand what has been occurring in Lebanon since the cease-fire that came into effect on the early hours of August 14, we must analyze the war's real aims, designed in concert with the United States and backed by it. In short, we need to take a close look at the actual unfolding of Israel's offensive, as its official aims were very much blurred.[1]

The Real Aims of Israel's Offensive

The central goal of the Israeli onslaught was, of course, to destroy Hezbollah. Israel sought to achieve this goal through the combination of three tactics.

The first consisted of dealing Hezbollah a fatal blow through a bombing campaign exploiting Israel's "overwhelming and asymmetric advantage" in firepower – as this kind of advantage is called in the jargon of the Pentagon, whose strategic options the Israeli general staff has copied. The campaign aimed at cutting Hezbollah's supply routes, destroying much of its military infrastructure (stocks of rockets, rocket launchers, etc.), eliminating a large number of its fighters, and decapitating it by assassinating Hassan Nasrallah and other key party leaders.

The second tactic consisted of turning Hezbollah's mass base among Lebanese Shiites against the party, which Israel then designated as responsible for their tragedy. This involved a frenzied military "psychological" campaign, including airdrops of leaflets, which everybody in Lebanon agreed were very clumsily written. In order to hammer this message through, Israel, of course, inflicted a disaster on the Lebanese Shiites through an extensive and devastating bombing campaign that deliberately flattened whole villages and neighborhoods and killed hundreds and hundreds of civilians.

This was not the first time Israel resorted to such a stratagem – a standard war crime according to international law. When the PLO was active in southern Lebanon, in what was called "Fatahland" before the first Israeli invasion in 1978, Israel heavily pounded the inhabited area around the point from which a rocket was launched at its territory, even though rockets were fired from wastelands. At that time, the stratagem succeeded in alienating from the PLO a significant part of the population of southern Lebanon, aided by the fact that quasi-feudal reactionary leaders were still a major force down there and Palestinian guerillas could easily be repudiated as alien since their behavior was often disastrous. During the Thirty-Three-Day War, given the incomparably better status of Hezbollah among Lebanese Shiites, Israel thought that it could achieve the same effect simply by dramatically increasing the scope and brutality of the collective punishment.

The third tactic consisted of massively and gravely disrupting the lives of the Lebanese people themselves and holding them hostage through air, sea, and land blockades. The aim was to incite this population, especially the non-Shiite communities, against Hezbollah, thereby creating a political climate conducive to military action by the Lebanese army against the Shiite organization. This is why, at the onset of the offensive, Israeli officials, including Prime Minister Olmert himself, stated that they did not want any force but the Lebanese army to deploy in southern Lebanon. They denigrated the existing UN force, the UNIFIL, while demanding the implementation of Security Council Resolution 1559 – a demand involving quite a bit of nerve on the part of a country holding the historical record for non-adherence to UN resolutions.

Measured against the central goal and these three schemes, the Israeli offensive was a total and blatant failure. The Israeli soldiers whom Hezbollah took as hostages (and whose liberation was the offensive's first official pretext) were not even released. And Hezbollah itself is far from destroyed: it has retained the bulk of both its political structure and its military force, indulging in its shelling of northern Israel up to the very last moment before the cease-fire on the morning of August 14. Not only has it not been cut off from its mass base, but this mass base has actually been considerably extended – among Lebanese Shiites as well as all other Lebanese religious communities, not to mention the huge international prestige that this war brought to Hezbollah, especially in the Arab region and the rest of the Muslim world.

Completing the picture is the fact that all this led to a shift in the overall balance of forces in Lebanon in a direction exactly opposite that expected by Washington and Israel: Hezbollah emerged much stronger and more feared by both its declared and its undeclared Lebanese opponents, the friends of the United States and the Saudi kingdom; and the Lebanese government seemed to side with Hezbollah, making the protest against the Israeli aggression its priority, thus conforming to the expectation of Lebanese public opinion. As an Israeli observer put it, in an article with a quite revealing title, "It was a mistake to believe that military pressure could generate a process whereby the Lebanese government would disarm Hizbullah."[2]

Taking Over from the Israeli Offensive

There is no need to dwell any further on Israel's most blatant failure: an avalanche of critical comments from Israeli sources has stressed the point. One of the sharpest comments was that expressed by three-time "defense" minister Moshe Arens, indisputably an expert. He wrote a short article in *Haaretz* that spoke volumes:

> They [Ehud Olmert, Amir Peretz, and Tzipi Livni] had a few days of glory when they still believed that the IAF's [Israeli Air Force's] bombing of Lebanon would make short shrift of Hezbollah and bring us victory without pain. But as the war they so grossly mismanaged wore on ... gradually the air went out of them. Here and there, they still let off some bellicose declarations, but they started looking for an exit – how to extricate themselves from the turn of events they were obviously incapable of managing. They grasped for straws, and what better straw than the United Nations Security Council. No need to score a military victory over Hezbollah. Let the UN declare a cease-fire, and Olmert, Peretz, and Livni can simply declare victory, whether you believe it or not ... The war, which according to our leaders was supposed to restore Israel's deterrent posture,

has within one month succeeded in destroying it.[3]

Arens spoke the truth: as Israel proved increasingly unable to score any of the goals that it had set for itself at the onset of its new war, its government started looking for an exit. As it was attempting to compensate for its failure through an escalation of the destructive and revengeful fury it had unleashed over Lebanon, its U.S. sponsors switched their attitude at the United Nations. After having bought time for Israel (indeed, more than three weeks) by blocking any attempt at discussing a Security Council resolution calling for a cease-fire – one of the most dramatic cases of paralysis in the history of the sixty-one-year-old intergovernmental institution – Washington decided to take over and continue Israel's war by diplomatic means.

The stalemate faced by the Israeli offensive, and the fact that Israel tried to make up for its failure by means of a murderous escalation that paradoxically bore witness to its impotence, resulted in a turnaround on the part of Washington's allies. After having attempted to put the blame on Hezbollah and Tehran, the United States' Arab allies – in particular, the tripartite axis composed of the Saudi kingdom, Egypt, and Jordan – became more and more worried about the turn of events, as Arab public opinion increasingly took up Hezbollah's cause. Washington's European allies, in turn, asked for the war to be stopped – too worried, themselves, about its repercussions, especially in countries with large Muslim immigrant communities.

Meanwhile, Tony Blair came under strong pressure from his own entourage.

Sharing with the United States a common, albeit rival, dedication to making the most of Saudi riches, especially by selling the Saudi rulers military hardware,[4] Paris regularly and opportunistically stays on the right side of Riyadh every time strains arise between Washington's agenda and the concerns of its oldest Middle Eastern clients and protégés. Israel's new Lebanon war offered precisely this opportunity: as soon as Israel's aggression proved counterproductive from the standpoint of the Saudi ruling family, who are terrified by the prospect of a popular explosion in the Middle East that could jeopardize their reign, they called for a cessation of the war and a switch to alternative means. The fact that their own Lebanese collaborators – Prime Minister Fuad Siniora, in particular – were begging for a cease-fire made their appeal all the more urgent.

Paris immediately came out in favor of this attitude, and Washington ended up following suit, but only after giving Israel a few more days to try to score a face-saving military achievement. The first draft resolution crafted by the two capitals circulated at the United Nations on August 5. It was too blatant an attempt at taking over from the unsuccessful Israeli offensive. The draft, while stating "strong support" for Lebanon's sovereignty, nevertheless called for the reopening of its airports and harbors only "for verifiably and purely civilian purposes" and provided for the establishment of an "international embargo on the sale or supply of arms and related material to Lebanon except as authorized by its government."[5]

The French–U.S. draft reasserted the need to implement Resolution 1559, calling for a further resolution that would authorize "under Chapter VII of the Charter the deployment of a UN-mandated international force to support the Lebanese armed forces and government in providing a secure environment and contribute to the implementation of a permanent cease-fire and a long-term solution." For all its vagueness, this formulation was paradoxically clear in implying a need for the creation of an international force authorized to wage military operations (Chapter VII of the UN Charter) in order to implement Resolution 1559 by force, in alliance with the Lebanese army.

Moreover, no provision restricted this future force to the area south of the Litani River, an area that, under the draft resolution, was to be free of Hezbollah's armament. (It also marked the limit of the zone that Israel ended up requesting to be secured after having failed to get rid of Hezbollah in the rest of Lebanon.) This meant that the new UN force could be called upon to act against the Shiite organization anywhere in Lebanon. All in all, the draft aimed at continuing Israel's action by means of a force acting under UN cover, which, for this reason, would have been able to deploy without facing resistance not only in the areas that Israel tried to invade but also in the rest of Lebanon.

This project was totally unwarranted by what Israel

had achieved on the ground, however, and the draft was therefore thwarted. Hezbollah came out strongly against it, clearly stating that it would not accept any international force but the existing UNIFIL, deployed along Lebanon's border with Israel (the "Blue Line") since 1978. The Lebanese government conveyed Hezbollah's opposition and request for change, backed by the chorus of Arab states including all U.S. clients. Washington had no choice, then, but to revise the draft, as it would not have passed a vote at the Security Council anyway.

Moreover, the principal European ally of the United States on the Lebanese issue, French President Jacques Chirac – whose country was expected by Washington to provide the major component of the international force and to lead it – had declared publicly two weeks into the fighting that no deployment would be possible without prior agreement with Hezbollah.[6] The Shiite organization's threat to oppose militarily any force dispatched under the conditions provided by the French–U.S. draft was sufficient to invalidate the latter.

Resolution 1701

The draft was therefore revised and renegotiated, while Washington asked Israel to brandish the threat of a major ground offensive and to start actually implementing it, as a means of pressure intended to enable the Bush administration to get the best possible deal at the Security

Council from their common standpoint. In order to facilitate an agreement leading to a cease-fire that became more and more urgent for humanitarian reasons, Hezbollah softened its position, accepting the deployment of 15,000 Lebanese troops south of the Litani River and the dispatch of more international troops to the same area in the framework of UNIFIL. Resolution 1701 could thus be pushed through at the Security Council on August 11.

The iniquity of this resolution is blatant. It fails to condemn Israel's criminal aggression, mentioning only "Hezbollah's attack on Israel" and the "hostilities in Lebanon and in Israel" [*sic*]. It demands that Israel cease its "offensive military operations" without even demanding the immediate lifting of the blockade that it was imposing on Lebanon – as if a blockade were not a particularly offensive military operation in itself. And, worse still, the new UNIFIL – which, remarkably, is deployed only on the territory of the occupied country – is supposed to ensure that its zone of deployment is not used for "hostile activities of any kind": Resolution 1701 says not a single word about the protection of Lebanese territory against the repeated aggression by Israel, an occupying power in Lebanon for eighteen years.

Washington and Paris's main concession was to abandon the project of creating an ad-hoc multinational force under Chapter VII of the UN Charter. Instead, the resolution authorizes "an increase in the force strength of UNIFIL to a maximum of 15,000 troops," thus revamping and considerably swelling the existing force. The main trick, however, was to redefine the mandate of this force so that it could now "assist the Lebanese armed forces in taking steps" toward "the establishment between the Blue Line and the Litani River of an area free of any armed personnel, assets and weapons other than those of the government of Lebanon and of UNIFIL." UNIFIL can now as well "take all necessary action in areas of deployment of its forces and as it deems within its capabilities, to ensure that its area of operations is not utilized for hostile activities of any kind."

Combined, these two precedent formulations come quite close to being a Chapter VII mandate – or, at any rate, could easily be interpreted this way. Moreover, the mandate of UNIFIL is actually extended by Resolution 1701 beyond its "areas of deployment," as it can now "assist the government of Lebanon at its request" in its effort to "secure its borders and other entry points to prevent the entry in Lebanon without its consent of arms or related materiel." This sentence clearly refers not to Lebanon's border with Israel but to its border with Syria, which runs the length of the country from north to south. What else could be the purpose of this excessive swelling of UNIFIL as a result of which, if and when it reaches its full size in addition to the 15,000 Lebanese soldiers, the area south of the Litani River will have the highest rate of soldiers to population in the world – that is, close to one soldier for every seven inhabitants![7]

These are the major time bombs included in Resolution 1701. Indeed, the spirit of the resolution is to treat Lebanon as if it were the aggressor! In this sense, it represents an attempt to continue the Israeli war in Lebanon in another fashion, which could imply war operations in the short or medium term. That is undoubtedly why the United States and Israel have so urgently insisted on the participation of NATO troops in the reinforced UNIFIL. What is developing is the replication of a practice symptomatic of the new times: the use of the United Nations as a fig leaf for military operations led by Washington along with NATO and other allies, as has been the case in Afghanistan since December 2001.[8]

Logically speaking, an interposition force should be made up of troops from neutral countries. Yet Washington and Paris are in no way neutral in the Lebanese conflict. No force formally allied to Washington – as is true of troops from all NATO member countries – can be considered neutral in a conflict between one of Washington's principal allies and another state. But the partiality of the European countries taking part in UNIFIL goes far beyond their membership in NATO.

France has collaborated closely with Washington on the Lebanese issue since 2004. Germany, which took upon itself the task of monitoring Lebanon's territorial waters, provides Israel with submarines, while Chancellor Angela Merkel has declared that the mission of the German fleet is to protect Israel. Italy is tied with Israel by an accord on military cooperation concluded by the government of Silvio Berlusconi in 2003 and ratified by the Italian parliament in 2005 with support from the Democratici di Sinistra led by the current Italian foreign minister, Massimo D'Alema.[9]

Hezbollah's Stance

The Shiite organization agreed to the Lebanese government's approval of the Security Council resolution. On August 12, Hassan Nasrallah gave a speech explaining the decision of his party to agree to the UN-mandated deployment. It included a much more sober assessment of the situation than that displayed in some of the speeches and statements he made during the fighting, as well as a good deal of political wisdom. "Today," Nasrallah said, "we face the *reasonable and possible* natural results of the great steadfastness that the Lebanese expressed from their various positions."[10] This soberness was necessary at a time when Lebanon was suffering the shock of Israel's devastating aggression. Any boastful claim of victory at this very moment[11] – such as those cheaply expressed at the same time by Hezbollah's backers in Tehran and Damascus – would have required Nasrallah to add, like King Pyrrhus of Ancient Greece, "One more such victory and I shall be lost!" Hezbollah's leader wisely and explicitly avoided engaging in a polemic about the assessment of the war's results, stressing that "our real priority" is to stop the aggression, recover the occupied territory, and "achieve security and stability in our country and the return of the refugees and displaced persons." He defined the position of his movement as follows: to abide by the cease-fire, and to fully cooperate with "all that can facilitate the return of our displaced and refugee people to their homes, to their houses, and all that can facilitate humanitarian and rescue operations."

Nasrallah did so while also expressing the readiness of his movement to continue the legitimate fight against the Israeli army as long as it would remain on Lebanese territory, though he offered to respect the 1996 agreement between his organization and Israel whereby operations of both sides would be restricted to military targets and spare civilians. In this regard, Nasrallah ensured that his movement had started shelling northern Israel only as a reaction to Israel's bombing of Lebanon after the July 12 operation, adding that Israel was to be blamed for deliberately extending the war to the civilians in the first place.

Hezbollah's chief then stated a position toward Resolution 1701 that could best be described as approval with many reservations, pending verification in practical implementation. He expressed his protest against the unfairness of the resolution, which refrained in its preambles from any condemnation of Israel's aggression and war crimes; but he also asserted that it could have been much worse and expressed his appreciation for the diplomatic efforts that prevented that from happening. His key aim was to stress the fact that Hezbollah considers some of the issues dealt with in the resolution to be Lebanese internal affairs that ought to be discussed and settled by the Lebanese themselves – to which he added an emphasis on the need to preserve Lebanese national unity and solidarity.

Hezbollah in fact had to make concessions under duress to facilitate the ending of the war. As the whole population of Lebanon was held hostage by Israel, any intransigent attitude would have had terrible humanitarian consequences beyond the already appalling results of Israel's destructive and murderous fury. Besides, Hezbollah knows perfectly well that the real issue is less the wording of the Security Council resolution than its actual interpretation and implementation, and that in this respect the real determinants are the situation and balance of forces on the ground. In response to George W. Bush's and Ehud Olmert's vain boasting about their victory as supposedly embodied in Resolution 1701, one need only quote Moshe Arens's pre-emptive reply in the above-cited article:

> The appropriate rhetoric has already started flying. So what if the whole world sees this diplomatic arrangement – which Israel agreed to while it was still receiving a daily dose of Hezbollah rockets – as a defeat suffered by Israel at the hands of a few thousand Hezbollah fighters? So what if nobody believes that an "emboldened" UNIFIL force will disarm Hezbollah, and that Hezbollah with thousands of rockets still in its arsenal and truly emboldened by this month's success against

the mighty Israel Defense Forces, will now become a partner for peace?[12]

The Continuation of War by Other Means

The "continuation of war by other means" started in full in Lebanon as soon as the cease-fire came into force. At stake are four main issues, reviewed here in the chronological order in which they came to the fore.

The first issue is, of course, the composition and mission of the new UNIFIL contingents. Israel vetoed the participation of troops from Arab or Muslim countries that do not maintain diplomatic relations with it, while Washington exerted strong pressure not only on Paris (in an effort to overcome the reluctance and apprehension of the French military) but also on its other NATO allies (urging them to send troops and hardware to Lebanon). Being no fool, Hezbollah tried to hamper as much as possible the execution of this first phase of what it perceived to be a new effort aiming at disarming it eventually, in the same spirit that presided over Resolution 1559 and in congruence with the Israeli offensive.

Hezbollah's effort to dissuade France from executing its plan of sending close to Lebanon's shores its single aircraft-carrier, which played a notable role in the bombing of Afghanistan alongside U.S. forces,[13] is what led to the French hesitation. But the international balance of forces did not allow Hezbollah to impose its own veto all the way, as Israel did, without incurring great risks. It therefore had to resign itself to the deployment of NATO forces in southern Lebanon and Lebanese territorial waters, but managed nonetheless, with help from Damascus, to prevent their stationing on the border between Lebanon and Syria.

The second issue is the "disarmament" of Hezbollah in the zone delimited in southern Lebanon for the joint deployment of the Lebanese army and the revamped UNIFIL. The most that Hezbollah conceded in this respect is to "hide" its weapons south of the Litani River – that is, to refrain from displaying them and to keep them in covert storage. In order to give up its arms in that area, as well as in the rest of Lebanon, Hezbollah laid down a set of conditions that start from Israel's evacuation of the Shebaa Farms area and end with the emergence in Lebanon of a government and army able and determined to defend the country's sovereignty against Israel.

The issue of Hezbollah's disarmament is, to be sure, the major stumbling block for Resolution 1701, as no country on earth is presently willing to try to disarm Hezbollah by force – a task that even the most formidable modern army in the whole Middle East and one of the world's major military powers has blatantly failed to achieve. This is indeed why Washington's aim is to prepare conditions under which the Lebanese army, commanded by the Lebanese allies of the United States, would be able to take the initiative in a new attempt at disarming Hezbollah, in which case NATO troops would come to

69

its aid as authorized by UNIFIL's new mandate.

The third issue is what could be called the "reconstruction battle." Rafic Hariri and his Saudi backers had built up their political influence in Lebanon by dominating the reconstruction efforts that followed Lebanon's fifteen-year civil war concluded in 1990. This time, the governmental majority is facing an intensive competition from Hezbollah, with both Iran's support and the advantage of the intimate link that the party has weaved with the Lebanese Shiite population, the principal target of Israel's war of revenge. As senior Israeli military analyst Ze'ev Schiff put it in *Haaretz* on the eve of the cease-fire: "A lot also depends on who will aid in the reconstruction of southern Lebanon; if it is done by Hezbollah, the Shiite population of the south will be indebted to Tehran. This should be prevented."[14]

But although this message was received loud and clear in Washington, Riyadh, and Beirut, Hezbollah has unquestionably won the first round of the battle by overtaking the Lebanese government and its international sponsors – notably thanks to Tehran's funding, which Ayatollah Khamenei himself pledged publicly to provide from the very beginning of the Thirty-Three-Day War.[15] With the Jihad al-Binaa (The [Re]Construction Jihad) that Hezbollah founded in 1988, following the model of its Iranian equivalent (Jihad-e Sazandegi, founded in 1979) and with its support, the Shiite organization has at its disposal a smoothly running structure toward that end. To deal with the most urgent needs – and in conformity with its religious tradition, which emphasizes charity over social demand – Hezbollah distributed bundles of banknotes to the families that have lost their housing. This occurred in a country where the proportion of vacant flats is particularly large due to high prices[16] – a situation that the founder of the Movement of the Deprived, Musa al-Sadr himself, had already denounced in a populist fashion at the beginning of the 1970s.[17]

The fourth issue, still on the domestic Lebanese level, is the fate of the cabinet. The existing parliamentary majority (the outcome of the elections held in Lebanon in 2005) resulted from elections flawed by a defective and distorting electoral law that the Syrian-dominated regime had enforced in 2000. One major consequence, as already stressed, was the distortion of the representation of the Christian constituencies, with great under-representation of the movement led by General Michel Aoun, who entered into an alliance with Hezbollah after the elections.[18] And what makes the legitimacy of the present parliamentary majority even more disputable is the profound effect of the recent war on the political mood of the Lebanese population. Of course, any change in Lebanon's government in favor of Hezbollah and its allies would radically alter the interpretation of Resolution 1701, as it depends very much on the Lebanese government's attitude.

Hezbollah and Michel Aoun have therefore jointly launched a campaign for political change according to the following timetable: enlargement of the Siniora government with the addition of followers of Aoun; drafting and promulgation of a new and fairer electoral law; organization of early elections; formation of a new government; and election by the new parliament of a new president of the republic. Aoun, of course, is the candidate for this latter office. The March 14 coalition, which currently holds the majority in parliament and government, has flatly refused these demands, thus contributing to the creation of a strong tension in the country – a tension that has increased the country's uncertainty over its future, both in the short and in the long run. Only one thing is certain: the offensive led by Washington in Lebanon since 2004, in line with which the Thirty-Three-Day War was a particularly devastating episode, is not close to conclusion.

In the alliance between Aoun and Hezbollah, the latter is much less reserved than the former. Indeed, General Aoun does not hesitate to criticize the Shiite organization, even though he praises the effectiveness of its resistance to Israel. Having never gone back on his resolute support for Resolution 1559 of 2004, which he claims to have co-authored, he still adheres to the objective of disarming Hezbollah, which he relates to the minimal conditions defined in the agreement document that they both signed on February 6, 2006:[19] liberation of the Shebaa Farms, release of the Lebanese prisoners detained in Israel, and definition of a defense strategy accepted by all the Lebanese. To put it clearly: Aoun will position himself as a providential man for Washington and Paris, and their Arab allies, when they realize that their present authorized allies in Lebanon are not able to subdue Hezbollah.

Lebanon stands again at a crossroads: a political settlement through the democratic way of holding new elections in the short term is reasonably the best alternative, the other one being a decision by the Aoun–Hezbollah alliance to resort to extra-parliamentary mobilizations that entail the risk of degenerating into new bloody clashes between the Lebanese. The Bush administration's frenzied interference in Lebanese affairs encourages the governmental majority to stiffen its attitude and aims at provoking a new Lebanese civil war with NATO's involvement. However, Iran's deterrence power at the regional level weighs on the attitude of the Saudi kingdom and hence on that of Paris. Riyadh tries therefore to calm things down, jointly with Nabih Berri, the leader of Amal, the Shiite movement allied with Hezbollah. These were the main factors in the Lebanese equation during October 2006.

The ball is in the court of the March 14 alliance. And one can only hope that the care of some to preserve Lebanon – a country devastated several times by the settlement of international and regional accounts on its territory – prevails over the eagerness of others to eliminate their opponents by force. This is an insane and disastrous goal in a country as heterogeneous as Lebanon: Those who made this choice in 1975, incited by Washington, paid a very heavy price.

The country as a whole suffered an even heavier toll.

FOUR

Israel, Between its "Second Lebanon War" and its Participation in Washington's "Global War"

It is particularly worthwhile to focus on the Israeli–Lebanese conflict in the framework of the broader conflict pitting Israel against the Arab world, as the broader conflict pertains to the core of Washington's "unlimited global war," and, in many ways, the former is a concrete expression and model for the latter. In its aims and its methods alike, the war Israel has waged on the Palestinians and against Lebanon as well as Israel's ambitions with regard to Iran and Syria are simultaneously a laboratory for the U.S. neoconservatives' global war strategy and its most advanced front. It is easy to see that the stakes in this conflict go far beyond the countries directly concerned.

The Israeli Side's Stated Aims

One of the major problems the attack on Lebanon raised in Israel resulted from the failure of Ehud Olmert's government to clearly define its aims, whether political or military. Many Israeli commentators and columnists raised the question of the fog enshrouding these objectives. This question naturally found itself at the heart of debates in the wake of the war, including those in various commissions of inquiry set up to investigate the situation.

The decision to launch an attack on Lebanon was made immediately after a Hezbollah commando unit captured two prisoners of war on July 12, 2006. As Tanya Reinhart wrote, "The speed at which everything happened (along with many other pieces of information) indicates that Israel has been waiting for a long time for 'the international conditions to ripen' for the massive war on Lebanon it has been planning."[1] It was no secret for anyone: Washington and Tel Aviv wanted a war against Hezbollah, and the July 12 operation gave them an ideal pretext.

It wasn't the first time the Lebanese resistance group had attempted to capture Israeli soldiers in order to exchange them for Lebanese held by Israel. The only thing new in the July 12 operation was its success, only a few days after a Palestinian commando unit had captured corporal Gilad Shalit at the Kerem Shalom post, near the Gaza Strip.

Two kidnappings in a row were too much for Israel, which was losing face. The initial objective appeared then to be freeing its soldiers; in any case, that is what government spokespersons announced. However, as many commentators immediately pointed out, there was reason to wonder how such massive and murderous bombings could lead to the freeing of Israeli prisoners of war.

The second argument made by those close to the prime minister might appear more plausible: Israel wanted to force Lebanon to compel Hezbollah to hand over the Israeli soldiers unconditionally. The working hypothesis was classically colonial in the most banal sense: Hit the Lebanese state and people as hard as possible and they, "who, like all Arabs, only understand the language of force," would turn against Hezbollah in order to halt the massacre. This seemed even more likely when, in the words of a radio commentator, "There is a Christian majority [*sic*] in Lebanon, which hates Muslims, and Hezbollah in particular." This mixture of factual ignorance and misunderstanding of human behavior is staggering.

To launch an all-out attack on the whole Lebanese people, destroy a significant part of Lebanon's infrastructure (Beirut's port and international airport, hundreds of roads and bridges, a major electric power station, etc.), provoke the exodus of almost 1 million refugees in a matter of days, destroy dozens of villages and the southern districts of the capital, and massacre several hundred civilians, including civilians fleeing combat zones on Israeli army orders – to commit all these crimes in the belief that Lebanese resentment would turn against the Hezbollah militias, and not the Israeli army, is to engage in a particularly bad case of ideological blindness.

When it became clear that achieving the first stated objective – freeing two prisoners of war – was impossible, a new one was announced: the destruction of Hezbollah. But very soon, despite the tons of bombs showered on Lebanon, the Islamic Resistance continued to stand firm and gave no signs of caving in or being crushed. Day by day, the number of rockets hitting the north of Israel grew, including strikes against Haifa, Israel's third-largest city. Twice, Israeli authorities cried victory before the outcome was certain. They announced the death of Hassan Nasrallah, described as "buried under the ruins of his bunker," and then they announced the destruction of the organization's operational command. In reality, the massive bombings throughout Lebanon's entire territory failed even to put a dent in Hezbollah's operational capacities, with the possible exception of its long-range missiles, as a significant number was said to have been destroyed by Israeli aviation on the second week of the conflict.

As a result, the official objective was revised for the third time – and on this occasion, narrowed down. Specifically, it became limited to preventing missiles or other rockets from continuing to hit Israeli towns and villages. But Hezbollah was able to continue to pound the north of Israel until the last day of the war. Finally, after failing to achieve the set of objectives described above, the government decided to continue its war with the sole purpose of restoring the Israeli army's deterrent capacities, shaken by the Hezbollah combatants' effective resistance to the offensive. Starting then, Israel launched a no-holds-barred onslaught, launching hundreds of tons of bombs, including phosphorous bombs and cluster bombs, and destroying entire villages, to show the world that Israel remained a formidable military power. In this respect above all others, the Israeli war concluded as a fiasco.

So what remains for those who want to persuade themselves that the war was not a failure? According to Yoel Marcus, one of the leading *Haaretz* editorialists, "there's some good news underneath it all" – namely, that "Hassan Nasrallah and his deputy, who expected Israel to respond in a limited way, maybe three days at most, were stunned by the tremendous damage we inflicted over the course of six weeks. This surprise is a good thing, not least because of the lesson to be learned here: Israel is indeed unpredictable and is liable to go wild when it sees red."[2]

The dogged determination to keep up at any cost a military adventure doomed to failure can actually be explained by the prevalence of what Israeli writer Yitzhak Laor refers to as "military thought," following in the footsteps of pompous fools in the history of colonial warfare, from the French Massu to the American Westmoreland: "Give me two weeks more, and I'll crush them this time." And, without a doubt, the Israeli General Staff went far beyond acting as a simple lobby in this war; it was more like a parallel government. Yet this factor, however important it might be, has to be viewed as complementing another, political in nature: the structural integration of Israeli strategy into Washington's "unlimited global war," and the role U.S. leaders have assigned to Israel in this framework.

Israel in Washington's "Global War"

The wars Israel is waging nowadays can be seen as part and parcel of the permanent, preventive global war planned by the neoconservatives and launched by the White House after 9/11, with the increasingly generalized backing of the European Union. Of course, the state of Israel has always been in the military service of one or another Western power – the United States since the late 1960s – in exchange for economic, military, and diplomatic support. But these alliances have been based, overall, on a conjunction of interests: Israel was a bridgehead for the defense of the interests of the "free world" in the Middle East against the Soviet Union and Arab nationalism. In exchange, Western powers supported the state of Israel and its colonial project.

However, this mutual assistance pact did not always go smoothly, as the Zionist state's particular interests sometimes contradicted the global interests of one or another of the major powers. This was the case, for example, in 1956, when the United States forced Israel, as well as France and Great Britain, to withdraw from the Suez Canal and the Sinai. And again in 1991, George Bush Sr. suspended bank guarantees granted to Israel because the Shamir government refused to announce a freeze on settlements. Israel has often been the *enfant terrible* of the Western camp. Of course it was fully part of this camp, and sometimes played a central role in it, but at certain times it risked destabilizing the side's global interests, provoking a degree of tension in its relations with strategic allies.

"Unlimited global war" is a strategy that was conceived and prepared, in the 1980s, by U.S. and Israeli neoconservatives who were rethinking the post-Soviet-era world. The new strategy was a class war on a planetary scale, the aim of which was recolonization of the world and the imposition of a new imperial system governed by neoliberalism. Unilateralism was to replace the multilateral order laid out after World War II. Recolonization and imposition of U.S. hegemony were to put an end to peoples' self-determination, and unlimited war would replace the commitment to a political solution to crises as a means of achieving global security.

The convergence of Israeli and U.S. wars could not fail to spark debate as to whether Israel was waging its wars on behalf of its U.S. sponsor, or, on the contrary, if the United States was being swept along by Israel and its expansionist ambitions. During Condoleezza Rice's many visits to Jerusalem in August 2006, the prevailing view in the media, and among Israeli antiwar activists, was that the U.S. secretary of state was attempting to force Ehud Olmert's hand and make it understood that Washington expected Tel Aviv to do the job expected of it. Indeed, even the most hawkish U.S. neoconservatives expressed their discontent with the way Israel was waging the war

– especially with the fact that certain Israeli leaders were in favor of pulling out from what was proving more and more a fiasco.

Hezbollah "is today the leading edge of an aggressive, nuclear-hungry Iran," wrote *Washington Post* columnist Charles Krauthammer, a neoconservative very close to Dick Cheney. "America wants, America needs, a decisive Hezbollah defeat." However, "[t]here is fierce debate in the United States about whether, in the post–September 11 world, Israel is a net asset or liability. Hezbollah's unprovoked attack on July 12 provided Israel the extraordinary opportunity to demonstrate its utility by making a major contribution to America's war on terrorism." But Olmert's "search for victory on the cheap has jeopardized not just the Lebanon operation but America's confidence in Israel as well. That confidence – and the relationship it reinforces – is as important to Israel's survival as its own army. The tremulous Olmert seems not to have a clue."[3]

However, though it is true that the White House and above all the Pentagon were disappointed by the Israeli army's shabby performance in Lebanon, viewing Israel as a simple mercenary for imperial war does not correspond to reality. The "global war" is a strategy thought up by neoconservatives from both countries. As soon as they were in power in Tel Aviv and Washington, they found themselves in a true symbiosis, in thoughts as well as deeds. The fact that the Israeli neoconservatives came to power five years earlier than their North American co-thinkers

– after the November 1995 assassination of Yitzhak Rabin – may even create the impression that the Israelis have been setting the tone.

The all-out anti-terrorist discourse, transforming Palestinian victims into a threat looming over Israel, the renewed denunciation of Yasir Arafat as a terrorist leader, the desire to "reconquer" the Palestinian territories, the military methods used, and the concept of unlimited war were all tested in the Israeli-occupied territories before they were adopted by the United States, once Bush and his team came to power. But this process involved a daily dialogue between the members of Netanyahu team (most of them American Jews) and the Republican right wing, when it was still in the opposition. With George W. Bush's victory, there was a kind of merger of the policies of both states. It is not a matter of the dog wagging the tail, still less of the tail wagging the dog. Rather, a two-headed monster had emerged, though of course one head was bigger and wealthier than the other.

"Civilization War"

If there is any country where the "clash of civilizations" has become an official ideology that also comes close to permeating the entire society, it is certainly Israel. "We still live in a modern and prosperous villa in the middle of the jungle," declared former Prime Minister Ehud Barak in 1996, when he was still minister of foreign affairs.[4] This image is a perfect reflection of how Israelis view themselves in the heart of the Arab and Muslim world, as an outpost of civilization in the midst of a barbarous world whose only aim is the destruction of civilization and against which an unlimited preventive war is a matter of life and death.

For the various neoconservative governments that have ruled in Jerusalem, the preventive war is a war for survival. As such, it can have no limits – in terms of time but also in terms of means. The distinguishing feature of "civilization wars" and other crusades is the way they view the adversary – including civilians, of course – as a target to eradicate, or at least to utterly neutralize. It's "them or us." The war of destruction Israel has waged against Palestine since 2000 – but planned and prepared two years earlier – is the archetype of such new wars. Its bloody brutality is not "collateral" but intrinsic to its nature as a "civilization war," as are the destruction of Iraq and the more than 100,000 deaths resulting from the U.S. occupation.

Throughout the Thirty-Three-Day War against Lebanon, Israeli leaders, as well as the country's journalists and experts, spoke about "cultures" and a basic incompatibility between "us" – Israelis, but also Civilization with a capital C, which is assumed to be Judeo–Christian – and "them." This involves an utterly contradictory line of argument, incidentally. On the one hand "those people don't care if they die" or if they sustain casualties, whereas on the other hand the aim of the war and the massive destruction was to "teach them once and for all" what it would cost them to dare to attack Israel.

The Middle East is a central, priority objective in Washington's unlimited, preventive global war. In consequence, Israel's military role is more indispensable than ever before. For the Jewish state, it was a matter of both taming and "pacifying" rebellious peoples and of terrorizing others, so they would never dream of escaping U.S. hegemony or countering Israel's own aims. The martyrdom of Gaza and the deliberate destruction of Lebanon are both aspects of this "pacification" and terror policy.

These elements convey some idea of how weak the risks of tensions between Israeli militarism and what is commonly called the "international community" really are. True, the latter may at times try to put a damper on Tel Aviv's martial ambitions – when these ambitions run the risk of fanning a spirit of revolt throughout the region, as was the case during the most recent Israeli operation in Lebanon. And it is precisely because Hezbollah's resistance has undermined the Zionist state's dissuasive capacity that Israel is now programming a second round.

Military Failure

As early as the second week of the war, journalists in Israel and pro-Israeli journalists abroad were not hesitating to criticize how it was waged, while a large majority among Israeli public opinion was supporting the military adventure in Lebanon. On July 22, the *New York Post* military analyst wrote: "Israel is losing this war. For a lifelong Israel supporter, that's a painful thing to write. But it's true. And the situation's worsening each day."[5]

No one doubts any longer that the Israeli operation in Lebanon was a failure. Even the White House – although it continues to go through the motions of speaking of success, hoping to calm down Pentagon and State Department officials who would like to put a damper on George W. Bush's uncritical backing of Israel, and even on some of the neoconservatives' blind following of flagrantly irresponsible policies. The best evidence of failure is the impressive number of commissions of inquiry set up in Israel, some of them under public pressure.

It was first and foremost a failure of intelligence services that had always been viewed, mistakenly, as the best in the world. These services may be high performance at carrying out commando operations, kidnappings, and extrajudicial killings, but in terms of intelligence as such, their performance was pitiful once again.

The key word of this war, in fact, is "surprise." The Israeli government was taken by surprise by Hezbollah's ability to fight back and by its effective defense system on the border. It was surprised by the quantity of missiles and other rockets capable of hitting the north of Israel and by the antitank weapons that shattered the myth of the indestructible Israeli Merkava IV tank. It was taken by surprise, above all, by Hezbollah combatants' high level of efficiency and motivation. In short, it was surprised by everything that makes the difference between an obvious victory and a probable defeat.

Former military intelligence chief Brigadier General Yossi Kuperwasser may well have said, "I was absolutely not surprised," and "This is exactly the Hezbollah I know," but he was unable to convince the journalist interviewing him. "Then why is there a powerful feeling among the public that the political and military echelons were caught with their pants down?"[6] Indeed, the real question is not whether Aman or Mossad had factual information about Hezbollah but, rather, whether they have the political capacity to analyze such data and especially to draw the right conclusions from it.

And yet this is not the first time Israeli intelligence was caught with its pants down: it was surprised in 1973 by the large-scale offensive launched by the Egyptian and Syrian armies. It was surprised in 1982 by the Lebanese–Palestinian forces' ability to resist Israeli aggression and by the complexity of the Lebanese political scene where Sharon's plans got pathetically bogged down. Israeli intelligence was caught out by the first Intifada in 1987, then by Yasir Arafat's refusal to give in to Ehud Barak's diktat at Camp David in the summer of 2000, and surprised yet again by the Hamas victory in January 2006, although Israel had done everything to provoke it. And the list goes on.

This inability to understand the adversary and thus to anticipate its reactions is typical of the colonial relation. It has been repeated in all colonial adventures in modern history. The colonized group – in the case concerning us here, a group toward which the colonizer has a feeling of cultural superiority, as its constituents belong to a civilization whose characteristics and motivations have been determined in advance – no longer needs to be studied. The colonized group is what the colonizer says it is, unchanging and predetermined by the traits that are part of the very nature of its status.

The Arab is primitive and cowardly, the Muslim cruel and anti-Semitic. We, Israelis, are civilized, modern, and efficient and can even display generosity at times. There is no need to look deeper. It is the "modern and prosperous villa in the middle of the jungle," the war for civilization against barbarism. "The common denominator of all the failures" of the Intelligence services, writes Uri Avnery, "is the disdain for Arabs, a contempt that has dire consequences. It has caused total misunderstanding, a kind of blindness of Hezbollah's motives, attitudes, standing in Lebanese society, etc." [7]

However, reality has never corresponded to this colonial line. On the opposite side, the colonized group, owing to its very weakness with respect to the colonizer, has had to make the effort to know its enemy in order to survive. In general, it manages to do so. One need only see how Palestinians have learned to know the Israelis, their mentality, the contradictions within Israeli society. They have learned how to judge the soldier at a checkpoint at a glance: Russian or Moroccan, crabby or cool – and to draw snap conclusions from these clues: attempt to cross, or turn back and try their chances at another checkpoint.

For their very survival, the colonized become wiser while the colonial forces, sure of their superiority, let matters go. As a result, they are "taken by surprise" and run more and more risks of failing in their undertaking.

Another error typical of colonial rule, repeated in Lebanon: just rely on the big stick – in the case we are looking at here, thousands of bombs – and the adversary will learn to behave properly and accept whatever we want them to do or refrain from doing. According to colonialist reasoning, the Lebanese people, subjected to a hail of bombs, could not help but rise up against Hezbollah, supposedly to blame for everything that happened to them. A grave error: the Lebanese people united against those who were destroying their country.

The Israeli military failure thus resulted as much from the Hezbollah fighters' effectiveness and the Lebanese people's ability to resist as from the grave deterioration of the Israeli army and its operational abilities. We do not need any commissions of inquiry to learn the causes of this deterioration, of which we can identify three.

The first relates of course to the reason Israeli institutions have proven unable, once again, to anticipate the Lebanese reaction to their offensive – in other words, it relates to colonial arrogance. Over the years, racist contempt for Arabs and the army's superiority complex have meant that the army has gone to no particular effort to develop its own organizational capacities. All the reservists mobilized for the Lebanon war confirm this: they had not undergone any serious training in years, and their equipment was obsolete and ill-adapted to the war they were called upon to fight.

The General Staff, headed by an aviator for the first time in its history, relied on the total supremacy of air power, neglecting preparations for the land army. However, as the United States learned to its sorrow, it is impossible to subject a people and break its will to resist solely by relying on air power. An intervention by the land army is indispensable at one stage or another of a war. And like their U.S. counterparts, the Israeli tank units and infantry were not prepared for a war against well-trained, well-armed partisan units. They were unable to achieve a single one of their operational objectives.

Which leads us to the second reason for the deterioration of the Israeli army's effectiveness: for over five years, Israeli troops had been waging "war" on civilians, clamping down on women and children, attacking civilian objectives on the West Bank and the Gaza Strip, facing an unarmed population or very poorly trained and poorly armed combatants. The army persists in calling this massive police clampdown operation a "war." Often, during anti-occupation demonstrations, anti-colonial activists have mocked soldiers, warning them of the confusion between unilateral repression and war: "The day you face well-armed and trained adversaries, you'll be at a loss about what to do!" This is precisely what has happened in Lebanon: used to unilateral brutality, Israeli troops found themselves at a loss against well-trained combatants.

Neoliberal War

The news in the Israeli press that Chief of Staff Dan Halutz sold off all his stock market shares at the beginning of the crisis, knowing that their value would probably fall soon, is very revelatory of the nature of this war. In the neoliberal era, officers no longer seek glory and military success, but look at ways to make still more money. While still under arms, they are already preparing their second career, which is often in the field of arms trafficking or the sale of security systems to Latin American dictatorships or drug traffickers.

Thus we come to the third cause: Israel's failure in the Thirty-Three-Day War was the result of the grave deterioration of the preparedness of the military staff, who, like their chief, were more interested in stock market fluctuations than in the readiness of their troops. Worse still, the multiplication of bribery scandals seems to have contributed to poor-quality equipment in certain units. It appears that certain officers agreed – in exchange for sizeable payments under the counter – to buy such-and-such item of equipment rather than another, despite its questionable quality.

Neoliberalism bears war as storm clouds bear rain; but, paradoxically, it also comes into tension with the requisites of war. Individual quests for maximum profit, dismantlement of public services, and generalized privatization are frequently at loggerheads with "the national interest" and patriotism, because it is impossible to seek individual profit and serve the general interest at the same time, even in war.

A characteristic of this tension is the lack of preparedness among services intended to help civilians in wartime, such as inadequate civil defense shelters and supplies for people locked down in these shelters during bomb alerts. This structural deficiency is even more serious because modern war increasingly targets civilians. Questioned by Israeli radio about the serious failings of municipal services assisting civilians who had taken refuge in shelters for weeks on end, an aide to Haifa's mayor replied: "It is true that the municipality has not done much, but there are NGOs to pick up the slack." Dismantling public services, privatizing charity – that is how the neoliberal state and its institutions wage modern war, by offloading their responsibilities to NGOs. These often do remarkable work, but they can never substitute for the state and its institutions in providing citizens the help they are entitled to.

In an article titled "Betrayed by the State," Daniel Ben Simon, one of the best Israeli journalists, wrote, without hiding his rage:

> All the committees of inquiry that will be set up cannot atone for the real crime that took place before our very eyes during the second Lebanon War. The state simply disappeared, as if the earth had opened up and swallowed it. It was not present in northern towns at the

toughest moments for those residents who stayed in their homes. The substance of the state is tested during moments of trial. In this test, Israel failed.

The corpses that continued to float in New Orleans days after Hurricane Katrina subsided revealed the true face of the United States. This enormous power displayed helplessness more appropriate to Bangladesh. President George Bush, so quick on the draw when it comes to war, let four days go by before he visited Louisiana.

Katrina exposed the weakness of an ideology that preaches weakening the state in favor of private economic organizations in a free market economy ...

That is what happened to northern towns during the war.[8]

The abandonment of the citizenry was all the more noticeable in this war, in comparison to all previous wars since 1956, because the Israeli civilian population was targeted and hard hit. Until this war, only people in Arab countries had suffered in wars with Israel – except in a few rare cases, as when Palestinian rockets hit Israeli towns in the 1970s and 1980s.

When they bombed the southern districts of Beirut from the first day of the war and pounded dozens of towns and villages in southern Lebanon, the Israeli authorities knew – or should have known, had they paid attention to Hassan Nasrallah's speeches – that Hezbollah would hit back by bombing Israeli towns. Not only were all places in northern Galilee hit, with relatively few victims and a great deal of damage, but Haifa itself, the third-largest city in the country and its major industrial center, was bombed until the last day of the hostilities.

Hundreds of buildings were destroyed and more than a half-million Israelis had to seek refuge in the center of the country. Those who were unable to leave, generally the poorest, were completely forsaken by the state. One of those who came to their rescue was Arcadi Gaydamak, a billionaire of Russian origin, thereby considerably improving his rather dubious reputation. Government indifference to the civilian population was indeed one of the most important factors in the public demand for a commission of inquiry. However, we can safely bet that this commission of inquiry will not waste much time on the utter lack of means of protection (shelters, alarm sirens, etc.) in Arab localities in Israel. This discrimination is so structural that nobody beyond the people affected pays any attention to it or feels any outrage. It also partly accounts for the fact that the majority of Israeli civilian victims were Arabs. Of course, there is an Arab majority in the northern part of Israel, but not in the same proportion.

The 1,500 Lebanese civilian victims and approximately 40 Israeli civilian victims were not "collateral damage" in this war. One can never repeat it enough: attacks on civilians and the destruction of dwellings and civil infrastructure are intrinsic to the "global war on terrorism" now under way, which knows no limits. The rules of warfare as defined by the international community following the 1945 victory over fascism have become null and void in the eyes and statements of the U.S. president himself.

In this war, the enemy is no longer an army or a nation's economic might but, rather, the nation itself, identified with the terrorist plague that must be eradicated. The neoconservative strategy has evolved from the war against terrorist networks into a war on terrorist states (the so-called "rogue states"), concluding with a war on entire peoples viewed as terrorists because they tolerate the actions of terrorists in their midst or the continuation of a regime defined as terrorist. According to this logic, it has become legitimate to attack peoples themselves, whether in Afghanistan, in Iraq, in the occupied Palestinian territories, or in Lebanon.

Antiwar Movements

The previous Israeli war on Lebanon, launched in 1982, gave rise to the emergence of a powerful antiwar movement in Israel. Within six months, this movement succeeded in winning over a majority of public opinion. This time, there was no mass opposition to the war against Lebanon. The obvious question is: why not?

In 1982, the Israeli government decided to wage war on Lebanon to achieve objectives of deep concern to the Zionist state and its Lebanese allies: expelling the Palestinian resistance and putting the Maronite right wing in power. Although Washington had given Begin and Ariel Sharon a green light, its support was conditional. The U.S. administration did not take long to link up with the European states in their attempt to moderate and finally call a halt to the Israeli aggression, out of fear of the regional and worldwide consequences. This growing pressure from the "international community" was one of two key factors that made possible the emergence of a mass antiwar movement in Israel. The other was the increasingly high cost this war was exacting on Israeli society, particularly in terms of the number of casualties.

The Israeli peace movement has always been motivated by the first of these factors: the cost – in terms of human lives, money, and social disruption – of wars not clearly viewed as self-defense. But this is not peculiar to Israeli society. The high cost of colonial wars has been responsible throughout history for turning public opinion around, in conflicts ranging from the Algerian War to the Vietnam War. The second factor is more specific to Israel – namely, fear of the loss of international support, particularly support from the United States.

During the Thirty-Three-Day War, neither of these factors came into play. In this connection, bear in mind that Israeli public opinion has undergone a radical change over time, in three stages. In July 2000, there was Ehud Barak's big lie about Yasir Arafat's rejection of his "generous offer," compounded by his assertion that he had unmasked the Palestinian leadership's "real intentions" – to "throw the Jews in the sea" – hidden behind a moderate discourse and an apparent willingness to compromise. Then, in September 2000, came the popular response to Ariel Sharon's provocation, which "confirmed" the Palestinian plan to eradicate Israel. Finally, September 11, 2001, made it possible to enroll the Israeli "war of self-defense" in the global war against militant Islam that threatens not only Israel but all "Civilization."

From this outlook, the Zionist state found itself engaged in a war of survival against the Islamist terrorist menace. In a war of this type, the victims (Israeli victims – the only ones that matter to the Zionists) are not the consequence of a militaristic policy that could have and should have been averted for this very reason, but the inevitable price to pay for self-defense. Thus, there is no chance that the forces comprising the Israeli peace movement during the first Lebanon war will take to the streets once again. The war that Israel has waged since September 2000 against the Palestinian people and the war launched against Lebanon in the summer of 2006 are both aspects of the war being waged by the "civilized world" against international terrorism, and the respectable Israeli left need not fear that its state will fall out of tune with the "international community."

This perception of Israel and its wars – which is of course linked to the fact that, contrary to the case during the 1982 Lebanon war, the Labor Party was in government in 2000 and 2006 – put the peace movement, as of July 2000, into a deep coma. Its most prestigious spokespersons supported Israeli aggression and war crimes in the occupied Palestinian territories and in Lebanon.

And it is not by chance that the 5,000 demonstrators shouting "No War" in the Tel Aviv streets during July and August 2006 were the same people who mobilized against Israeli army exactions in the occupied territories. The unlimited war against terrorism is one and the same, whether waged in Ramallah in 2000, in Nablus in 2003, or in Beirut in 2006. Either we accept its outlook, or we reject it as a manipulative mystification cooked up by neoconservatives in New York and Tel Aviv and taken up little by little by the greater part of the rest of the "international community."

The Peace Now movement and the Labor left accepted this outlook, from July 2000 onward. As a result, they supported the invasion of Lebanon in 2006. Activists in Israeli anti-colonialist organizations, the Coalition of Women for a Just Peace, the Yesh Gvul refuseniks, Gush Shalom, Taayush, Anarchists Against the Wall, and a few other associations such as Rabbis for Human Rights and the Alternative Information Centre, refused to fall into this trap in 2000–2001. Accordingly, they were able to meet the challenge of the war against Lebanon in the summer of 2006.

We must recognize, however, that the courage and determination of these activists were not sufficient to make up for an absent mass antiwar movement. The Thirty-Three-Day War took place in a consensus atmosphere;

the vast majority of Israeli society backed the war, even after the high price paid by the Israeli public had become obvious to everyone. The hundred some Israeli deaths, the dwellings destroyed in the north of the country, and the hundreds of thousands of displaced persons were accepted by the Israeli population as the unavoidable price to be paid for a war of self-defense and survival.

After War, Crisis

On August 30, *Haaretz* columnist Uzi Benziman drew the balance sheet of the war:

> From the public's point of view, whoever brought upon the country the calamity of July–August must pay the piper.
>
> On the face of it, Olmert recognizes this. The person who describes himself as supremely responsible for going to war and for its results, and the person who created three committees to examine how it was conducted admits there were serious failures… .
>
> Olmert failed in setting the initial goals of the war, in comprehending the implications of the military moves, in the freedom of action he continued to grant the General Staff despite seeing before him how its expectations disintegrated, and in authorizing a ground

offensive on the eve of a cease-fire agreement. This is enough for any decent person to conclude that the position of prime minister is simply too much for him.[9]

This judgment is nearly unanimous in Israel. The war was a failure in both political and military terms, and Ehud Olmert and his Labor minister of defense, Amir Peretz, bear responsibility for this failure, along with the General Staff. This is why the demand for a national commission of inquiry is so widespread and more than 50,000 people demonstrated in September, in Tel Aviv, to impose it. Aware of the fact that such a commission would call upon government policy-makers to leave their places to others, as happened after the October 1973 war, Olmert and Peretz chose to avoid such an outcome by appointing various minor commissions of inquiry with a mission to analyze secondary aspects concerning the course of the war. None of these commissions has the prestige or the judicial authority of a national commission of inquiry.

Yet, as emphasized by the editorialist quoted above, the feelings of failure that the prime minister shares with public opinion can have dramatic consequences. For instance, such a mood could lead to a second round of war in relatively short order after the first:

What is worrisome about Olmert's latest statements is not only their haughtiness but also their motive. The prime minister unwittingly revealed his mood at present: He is haunted by the failure of the war in Lebanon and is trapped by an indomitable ambition to slough off the shame of this image. The state now needs a level-headed leader who is not subject to the traumas and failures of the war, one who can take a sober look at the diplomatic and security situation. The leaders who carry in their consciousness the fresh burns of the campaign and the disgrace it caused them personally are liable, even unconsciously, to subjugate the country's needs to selfish considerations of image.[10]

Despite the comfortable majority the government enjoys in parliament, and less than six months after its triumphal election, an end-of-regime mood is clearly prevalent in Israel. The most recent polls announced the collapse of Olmert's Kadima Party and a spectacular rise in Netanyahu's Likud Party, which had been squeezed out in the previous elections. Of course, Olmert can legitimately blame on his predecessors not only the military failure but also the total lack of structures and measures with which to take charge of the civilian population in the event of bombings. Nobody could logically expect a new government to solve in only three months problems that the previous governments had not tackled in an entire decade.

So why did the government go to war when it was evident that nothing had been seriously prepared, even on an operational level? To be sure, blame can always be leveled against the American neoconservatives who goaded Olmert into launching a proxy offensive against Iran's allies. But the main reason – let it be repeated – is the colonial arrogance brought on by the Israeli army's overwhelming military superiority, which led it to believe that everything could be solved by a big-stick policy.

After the failure of such a policy based on sheer brutality, the time has come for the Israeli political class to think about its war before waging it once again, because war is still the only basis for a consensus within this political class. The Thirty-Three-Day War had scarcely finished when the experts were already preparing for the next round. Military analyst Avraham Tal, for one, gives a very clear-eyed explanation of what strategists are thinking about the impending war:

> A war that has ended in a tie and without an agreement between the sides being signed is destined to flare up again, sooner or later. In the conflict between Israel and Iran, by means of its proxy, Hezbollah, neither side achieved its strategic aim. Therefore, the prime minister was correct in telling the Knesset that it is necessary to ensure that next time "things will be done better."
>
> How can this be ensured? One must start from the working assumption that the next confrontation will erupt relatively soon; for

purposes of the discussion, let us assume two years from the eruption of the previous confrontation and to act in all areas as though this will happen with absolute certainty. Possibly there will be another round in the format of the second Lebanon war, but we must prepare for the possibility of something larger and more dangerous: an all-out war with regular armies, including the army of a regional power.[11]

In Tal's view, the strategic enemy is Iran: this is the "regional power" against which Israel must prepare for "all-out war." Ze'ev Schiff, the military affairs expert at the Israeli daily *Haaretz*, echoes the same idea and draws a significant conclusion: peace must first be made with Syria.

Israel finds itself in a strange contradiction, strategically speaking. On the one hand, it repeatedly emphasizes that for the first time since the 1948 War of Independence it is facing an existential threat: the threat of Iran, which is developing nuclear weapons and is controlled by an extremist religious regime whose president is calling for the eradication of Israel. On the other hand, Israel continues to consider the battle against the Palestinians as its main front. This contradiction defies all logic.

We are in need of a strategic revolution. We

have to determine that the first and primary front is the battle to prevent the existential threat …

Israel's strategic interest is to remove Syria from the Iranian axis. There is no better way to create a barrier between Israel and Iran than peace with Syria. We should aspire to that.[12]

This may sound like the voice of common sense, but some U.S. neoconservatives and a part of the Israeli security establishment do not look kindly upon a détente with the Syrian regime. Far from it; they would prefer to see Israel attack Damascus first. In other words, if all Israeli leaders agree to prepare for war or, more precisely, actively prepare for the next war, they have not yet reached an agreement as to the objective: Syria or Iran, or Syria and then Iran. There are even those who dream of fighting Syria and Iran at the same time and, of course, those who call for another war against Hezbollah.

Two years in which to repair all the deficiencies that came to light during the latest military adventure in Lebanon? This rather lengthy period seems justified, given the structural problems besetting the army and the state, a deficit of almost two decades of arrogant lack of preparedness, and a reign of generalized incompetence. But in any case Washington, on the one hand, and the military caste's desire for vengeance, on the other, do not leave the government and the army any more time than that to get the war machine back in fighting form.

And yet, if there is one lesson to be drawn from the recent war on Lebanon, it is that the era of cheap and easy wars – for Israel, that is – is definitively behind us, and that whatever the balance of power, civilian populations risk bearing the brunt of the cost. In this era of unlimited war, they have become the hostages in the hands of the warmongers, as a "negligible" price to pay for the achievement of the hegemonic dreams of the U.S. empire and its faithful ally in the Middle East.

As South African Minister for Intelligence Services Ronnie Kasrils wrote a few days before the cease-fire decreed by the UN Security Council:

> By bombing Beirut, Israel's leaders knew there would be retaliation, just as when they carry out targeted assassinations to provoke reaction and wreck unwanted negotiations. To them the terror of their own citizens, fleeing south or hiding in their bomb shelters, is an acceptable part of their cynical calculations. As Tanya Reinhart, Israeli peace activist, observed: "For the Israeli military leadership, not only the Lebanese and the Palestinians, but also the Israelis, are just pawns in some big military vision."[13]

The Sinking Ship
of U.S. Imperial Designs

The defeat of Hezbollah would be a huge loss for Iran, both psychologically and strategically. Iran would lose its foothold in Lebanon. It would lose its major means to destabilize and inject itself into the heart of the Middle East. It would be shown to have vastly overreached in trying to establish itself as the regional superpower. The United States has gone far out on a limb to allow Israel to win and for all this to happen. It has counted on Israel's ability to do the job. It has been disappointed.

Charles Krauthammer[1]

But the administration now has to admit what anyone – including myself – who believed in the importance of getting Iraq right has to admit:

whether for Bush reasons or Arab reasons, it is not happening, and we can't throw more good lives after good lives ... But second best is leaving Iraq. Because the worst option – the one Iran loves – is for us to stay in Iraq, bleeding, and in easy range to be hit by Iran if we strike its nukes ... We need to deal with Iran and Syria, but from a position of strength – and that requires a broad coalition. The longer we maintain a unilateral failing strategy in Iraq, the harder it will be to build such a coalition, and the stronger the enemies of freedom will become.

Thomas Friedman[2]

On the same day of August 4, 2006, in the midst of Israel's war on Lebanon, two of the most famous columnists in the United States, both of whom supported the Bush administration's imperial drive in the Middle East, took note of the fact that its ship is sinking. With the resounding Lebanese fiasco of the summer of 2006, there can no longer be any doubt that what many had forecast long ago is proving absolutely true: the Bush administration will definitely go down in history as the clumsiest crew that ever stood at the helm of the American empire.

Cowboy Diplomacy

George W. Bush and the pillars of his administration have already secured their position in the collective memory as the grave-diggers of U.S. post–Cold War imperial ambitions: they accomplished the incomparable feat of squandering the most exceptional conditions favoring U.S. imperialism since 1980, when the other world colossus started crumbling. They also closed the unique window of opportunity that Charles Krauthammer referred to in 1990 as the "unipolar moment."[3] Both opportunities were wasted because Bush and his cronies were inspired by precisely the same imperial hubris that distinguished the likes of Krauthammer and Friedman.

The lead article in *Time*'s issue of July 17, 2006, published just before the start of Israel's new Lebanon war, heralded "the end of cowboy diplomacy." It took note of the obvious fact that "the Bush Doctrine foundered in the principal place the U.S. tried to apply it":

> Though no one in the White House openly questions Bush's decision to go to war in Iraq, some aides now acknowledge that it has come at a steep cost in military resources, public support and credibility abroad. The Administration is paying the bill every day as it tries to cope with other crises. Pursuing the forward-leaning foreign policy envisioned in the Bush Doctrine is nearly impossible at a time when the U.S. is trying to figure out how to extricate itself from Iraq. Around the world, both the U.S.'s friends and its adversaries are taking note – and in many cases, taking advantage – of the strains

on the superpower. If the toppling of Saddam Hussein marked the highwater mark of U.S. hegemony, the past three years have witnessed a steady erosion in Washington's ability to bend the world to its will.[4]

The authors' most serious grievance was stated as follows: "As it turns out, Iraq may prove to be not only the first but also the last laboratory for preventive war. Instead of deterring the rulers in Tehran and Pyongyang, the travails of the U.S. occupation may have emboldened those regimes in their quest to obtain nuclear weapons while constraining the U.S. military's ability to deter them."

This very bitter assessment was accompanied in the *Time* article by the same hope as shared by the large chorus of U.S. allies, protégés, and clients. For all of them, with the outstanding exception of the Israeli government, the fact that the most prominent neocons in the Bush administration – including Paul Wolfowitz, and Richard Perle before him – had been pushed aside nurtured the hope that a new salutary course in the administration's foreign policy was in gestation. The reshuffle that occurred during George W. Bush's second term – despite the exit of realist-in-chief Colin Powell, who, in any case, had only limited influence on the administration – seemed indeed to confirm the "twilight of the neocons" that some Clintonites had announced two years beforehand.[5] However, what the *Time* authors announced as marking the end of "cowboy diplomacy" – "a strategic makeover is evident in the ascendancy of Secretary of State Condoleezza Rice" – proved to be no more than wishful thinking almost as soon as it was printed, in light of the events that subsequently unfolded when Israel launched the most brutal aggression of its history. Cowboy diplomacy, it turned out, had just been replaced with cowgirl diplomacy – essentially the same.

True, Condoleezza Rice did her best to put some make-up on the face of the Bush administration's foreign policy, but there was no significant shift in substance. A pillar of this administration since its inception, Rice shares the same delusions of grandeur and folly of overreaching designs that characterize the rest of the team. Put in charge of the State Department for Bush's second term, she carried out her mission, which consisted primarily of sealing off the many leaks in the administration's foreign policy ship: it was indeed a mission impossible. The ship is sinking inexorably in the dark waters of the Iraqi oil slick.

Gulliver and the Lilliputians

With the capacity to knock down any other regular army on earth, a military expenditure that exceeds that of the nearly 200 states that constitute the rest of the world combined, and a military budget that exceeds the gross domestic product (GDP) of all other countries except the fourteen largest economies after the United States – the U.S. "hyperpower" nevertheless proved one more time in contemporary history that it is unable to control rebellious populations in poor countries. Evidently, all the sophisticated killing gadgetry that the Pentagon possesses is of very limited help for such a purpose. Controlling populations involves troops: it is the kind of industry where labor cannot be replaced with hardware. That, incidentally, is why dictatorships are relatively more at ease in this business, as they can mobilize at will from their populations and do not fear paying a high price in soldiers' lives.

The United States proved unable to control Vietnam with a much higher rate of occupation troops to inhabitants than has been the case in Iraq. To be sure, U.S. military power is much greater today than it was at the time of Vietnam. But there is one context in which this does not hold true, and it is the one most crucial for occupation endeavors: troops. The number of U.S. troops has been radically cut since Vietnam and the end of the Cold War. Inspired by a spirit typical of the capitalism of the automation age, the Pentagon believed that it could make up for the unreliability of human resources by depending heavily on sophisticated weaponry – what got pompously called the "revolution in military affairs." It thus entered the age of "post-heroic" wars, as an analyst of military affairs aptly characterized them.[6] The United States did not have to go to much trouble to "post-heroically" defeat the Iraqi army of Saddam Hussein. Controlling the Iraqi population "post-heroically," however, proved an altogether different challenge.

The United States has been steadily losing control over Iraq ever since the occupation settled down in 2003. It was confronted, on the one hand, by the unfolding of an armed insurgency in the country's Arab Sunni areas that proved impossible to quench with the limited number of occupation troops available. For if an invading army is not capable of exerting control over every single acre of inhabited territory, as local armed forces usually do, there is only one secure way to get rid of an armed insurgency moving within its popular constituency – "like a fish in water," as Mao Zedong once put it. This way consists, of course, in draining the pool. The options are either to commit genocide, as the Russian army has started to do in Chechnya; to displace the population into concentration camps, as the French colonial army started doing in Algeria; or to combine the two, as the United States tentatively practiced in Vietnam but could not carry to conclusion because the American population would not have tolerated it.

Regarding Iraq, the United States was faced, on the other hand, by a much graver problem, one that became clear by the beginning of 2004: the Bush administration had been induced – by its own foolishness and by the sales patter of some of the Pentagon's Iraqi friends and the stupid delusions of others – into believing that it could win the sympathy of a large chunk of Iraq's majority community, the Arab Shiites. This proved a total disaster as the clout of Iran-friendly Shiite fundamentalist organizations completely dwarfed whatever constituency Washington's friends could buy among Iraq's Shiites. The Bush administration was left with no alternative for its imperial design but the classical recipe of "divide and rule," trying to foster antagonism between the three main components of the Iraqi population, countering the Shiites with Arab Sunni forces in alliance with the Kurds. It ended up fueling Iraq's slide toward a civil war, thus aggravating the overall spectacle of its failure in controlling the country.[7]

There is no doubt that the way in which the American Gulliver got tied down by the Iraqi Lilliputians – not to mention the impending disaster in Afghanistan, where the Taliban are now the ones who encircle NATO troops instead of the reverse – has considerably emboldened Iran, the other Middle Eastern pillar of what George W. Bush labeled the "axis of evil" at the onset of the imperial expedition he launched in the wake of September 11.

The utterly defiant – nay, provocative – attitude of Iran against the U.S. colossus was made possible only because the latter proved in Iraq to stand on feet of clay. Tehran successfully countered the attempt by Washington's Arab clients to expand the sectarian feud from Iraq to the rest of the Arab region in order to isolate the Iranian regime as "Shiite" – a ploy that had been used with some measure of success after the Iranian revolution of 1979. Tehran countered it this time by outbidding all the Arab regimes in hostility toward Israel, thus building up its image as a champion of the pan-Islamic cause.

A key to Tehran's success is the alliance that it weaved with Hamas, the most popular embodiment of Sunni Islamic fundamentalism. This alliance was enhanced when Mohammed Mahdi Akef, the head of the Egyptian section of the Muslim Brotherhood – the largest section of this movement, of which Hamas is the Palestinian branch – came out openly in support of Iranian President Mahmoud Ahmadinejad's provocative anti-Israel statements in 2005. Hamas's accession to power through the January 2006 Palestinian election dealt a further blow to Washington's regional strategy. Tehran jubilated, outbidding again all its Arab rivals in supporting the new Palestinian government. It was at this point that Israel stepped in, seen from Washington as the likely savior of what otherwise had started looking more and more like an imperial Titanic.

Israel to the Rescue

One more time in four decades of strategic alliance between the U.S. sponsor and the Israeli champion, Washington, still believing in the Israelis' old reputation of infallible know-how in dealing with their Arab foes, unleashed its favorite proxy against those it deemed to be Iran's proxies – namely, Hamas and Hezbollah. What the Bush administration overlooked, however, is that Israel's reputation had already been eroded by its blatant failure in controlling the 1967– occupied Palestinian territories, and even more so by its Saigon-like withdrawal from southern Lebanon in 2000, after eighteen years of occupation. Israel had thus already met its own Vietnam in Lebanon. And like the Pentagon after Vietnam, Israel's war planners have shifted since Lebanon to a "post-heroic military policy," relying much more on their superior hardware than on their ground troops' fighting capability.

When it invaded Lebanon in 1982, Israel was chiefly fighting the PLO guerillas: in Lebanon, these were anything but "fish in water," as they had managed to alienate the Lebanese population through arrogant and clumsy behavior. The Lebanese resistance that gathered momentum from 1982 onward, and in which Hezbollah came to play the major role, was a completely different story: this was the Israeli army's first encounter with a truly popular armed resistance with lines of supplies on a terrain adequate for guerrilla warfare. Israel faced the same "draining the pool" dilemma as that described above and, like the United States in Vietnam, it was compelled to swallow the bitter cup of a withdrawal that was tantamount to defeat, as it was unable to meet the conditions of victory.

Their belief in the invincibility of their superior weaponry – with a hubris that was enhanced by the amateurship in military affairs of Olmert and Peretz, the present captains of their crew – led the Israelis to believe that they could force Hezbollah into capitulation, or push the Lebanese to the brink of a new civil war, by taking the whole of Lebanon hostage, destroying the country's civilian infrastructure, and pouring on its Shiite-populated areas a deluge of bombs. Israel deliberately flattened whole neighborhoods and villages, leaving an aftermath resembling that of World War II bombings – or the bombing of Fallujah in Iraq, in 2004, though on a much larger scale, and accordingly much more visible. Israel's new war on Lebanon displayed the murderous fury of an act of revenge against the only population that had managed to oblige it to withdraw unconditionally from an occupied territory.

The criminal behaviors of the Israeli armed forces in Lebanon, with regard to the international conventions defining what constitute war crimes, went beyond those that the United States perpetrated directly on a mass scale in its post-Vietnam military expeditions, whether in Iraq or in former Yugoslavia. In this respect, Israel's onslaught on Lebanon amounted to a peculiar instance of the so-called extraordinary rendition policy. As is well known, Washington has handed over individuals it wants "interrogated," far beyond the limits imposed by U.S. legislative constraints, to those among its allied governments who face no hindrance in the dirty business of torture. And it was in the same spirit that Washington entrusted to Israel the task of fighting Hezbollah, seen as a major piece in the regional counteroffensive against Iran – in the hope that Israel, without incurring much trouble, could do the dirty work of extirpating an organization that is deeply rooted among the population.

Shamelessly exploiting, once again, the horrible memory of the Nazi judeocide – an exploitation that reached new depths on the occasion of the ThirtyThree-Day War – Israel's leaders believed that they could thereby deflect any criticism from the Western powers (a.k.a. "the international community"). Although the resources for this exploitation are unmistakably being depleted with every new threshold in brutality that Israel crosses, it is still quite effective. Any other state in the world that attacked a neighboring country, deliberately committing war crimes in so concentrated a time period as Israel did in Lebanon in the summer of 2006, would have brought upon itself an outcry far more vigorous than the timid objection that "Israel somewhat overdid it."

But for all that, Israel's brutal aggression failed to achieve its aim. On the contrary, it proved to be what Ze'ev Sternhell described euphemistically as Israel's "most unsuccessful war."[8] Sternhell's analysis concluded with this bitter statement:

> It is frightening to think that those who decided to embark on the present war did not even dream of its outcome and its destructive consequences in almost every possible realm, of the political and psychological damage, the serious blow to the government's credibility, and yes – the killing of children in vain. The cynicism being demonstrated by government spokesmen, official and otherwise, including several military correspondents, in the face of the disaster suffered by the Lebanese, amazes even someone who has long since lost many of his youthful illusions.

The Side Effects of Colonial Wars

Far from inducing civil war among the Lebanese, Israel's aggression succeeded in uniting them, for as long as the bombing went on, in a common resentment against its murderous brutality. Far from forcing Hezbollah into surrender, it turned the Shiite Islamic fundamentalist organization into the most prestigious foe ever to confront Israel since it defeated Egypt in 1967, transforming Hezbollah's chief Nasrallah into the most popular Arab hero since Nasser. And far from facilitating the efforts by Washington and its Arab clients to more deeply drive a wedge between Sunnis and Shiites, it led many prominent mainstream Sunni preachers to proclaim open support for Hezbollah. Among them were preachers from within the Saudi kingdom – the ultimate humiliation for the Saudi ruling family. The Iraqis unanimously denounced the Israeli aggression, while Washington's most formidable Iraqi foe and Tehran's ally, Moqtada al-Sadr, seized the opportunity to organize another huge demonstration, matching the one he had organized against the occupation of his country on April 9, 2005.

Egyptian sociologist Saad Eddine Ibrahim – one of the rare democrats persecuted by an Arab regime allied with Washington that the United States defended against his persecutors – founded in Cairo the Ibn Khaldun Center for Development Studies, a research institute that, among other activities, carries out opinion polls. He summarized in the *Washington Post* the most striking result of a popularity survey that his institute conducted in August 2006 among 1,700 persons all over Egypt: Hassan Nasrallah "appears on 82 percent of responses, followed by Iranian President Mahmoud Ahmadinejad (73 percent), Khaled Meshal of Hamas (60 percent), Osama bin Laden (52 percent) and Mohammed Mahdi Akef of Egypt's Muslim Brotherhood (45 percent)."[9]

It is impossible to formulate a more damning verdict about the Bush administration's policy in the Middle East. This opinion survey shows well that, however the situation in Lebanon evolves, the Israeli rescue boat, instead of helping to raise the sinking ship of the U.S. empire, actually aggravated the shipwreck, and was even dragged down with it. One can only hope that it does not carry down along with it thousands of additional victims in the Middle East – as well as in the rest of the world, the West included.

Gone, indeed, is the time when metropolitan countries could lead a carefree life while their armies waged colonial expeditions. France's interference in the war between Iraq and Iran led to the 1986 terrorist attacks in Paris; its interference in the Algerian conflict led to the 1995 attacks. Russia's colonial expedition in Chechnya led to murderous attacks on Russian territory, including Moscow itself. The massive comeback of U.S. armed forces in the Arab-Iranian Gulf countries led to the terrible attacks of September 11, 2001. Spain's participation in Washington's wars in the Middle East led to those in Madrid on March 11, 2004. The United Kingdom's participation in the same wars led to the London attacks of July 7, 2005. An impressive number of other attempts at organizing attacks in the same capital cities, as well as in many other Western cities, have been thwarted.

How many more deaths and horrors have to happen before colonial wars, occupations, and interferences cease for good?

Notes

Notes to Chapter 1

1. Lebanon's independence was proclaimed in 1943, but it was only in 1946 that the last French colonial troops left the country.

2. Malcolm Kerr, *The Arab Cold War: Gamal 'Abd alNasir and His Rivals, 1958–1970* (London: Oxford University Press, 1971).

3. This was the conclusion reached by the sectarian census of 1932. (No sectarian census was organized after that one.)

4. Georges Naccache, "Deux négations ne font pas une nation," editorial, *L'Orient* (Beirut), March 10, 1949.

5. From the name of Gamal Abdel-Nasser, president of Egypt from 1954 until his death in 1970.

6. For an analysis of Hezbollah, see Chapter 2 of this volume.

7. Intelligence services – in reality, mafia-like apparatuses.

8. While France's energy bill continued to expand owing to rising oil prices – the Saudi kingdom being France's third-largest oil supplier in 2005 after Norway and Russia – Paris considerably increased its efforts to augment

exports to Middle East oil producers. French exports to the Saudi kingdom increased by more than 26 percent in 2005, putting the kingdom in third place behind the United Arab Emirates and Iran. At the same time, the Saudi kingdom is France's second-largest commercial partner in the Middle East after Turkey. In March 2006, Jacques Chirac visited Riyadh in the company of fourteen CEOs of major French firms, including Total, Dassault, and Thalès. Four months later, on July 21, 2006, at the end of a visit to France by Saudi crown prince and minister of defense Sultan bin Abdul-Aziz, Paris and Riyadh signed two agreements for military cooperation providing for the supply of important equipment priced at several billion euros. The first phase of these agreements calls for nearly one hundred helicopters as well as Airbus tanker aircraft and cannons, and if a later agreement is signed, the Saudis would also get Rafale fighter planes and Leclerc tanks. In addition, Paris is trying to sell them frigates and submarines, as well as a radar monitoring system (225 radars) costing 7 billion euros. It is worth noting that in 2004 the Saudi kingdom held the third-largest stockpile of direct foreign investment in France from Middle East sources, after Lebanon (!) and the UAE.

9. On Amal, see Chapter 2.

10. This topic is discussed in Chapter 3.

Notes to Chapter 2

1. Hezbollah's anti-Israeli discourse often glides from anti-Zionism toward anti-Judaism and is not free from anti-Semitic influences. On this issue and on Hezbollah's ideology in general, see Amal Saad-Ghorayeb, *Hizbu'llah: Politics and Religion* (London: Pluto Press, 2002).

2. Does one need to dwell on the profound difference in nature between a terrorist organization like al-Qaeda and a mass party like Hezbollah? To be sure, they are both variants of Islamic fundamentalism; but this label refers to

a common programmatic category within which there is at least as much diversity as there was in the past within "communism" – between, say, the Red Brigades and the Italian Communist Party, to consider just one example from the same country. Nevertheless, one could still find some anti-Communists who were maniacal enough to put both Italian organizations into the same "totalitarian" category, in the same way that George W. Bush today includes both al-Qaeda and Hezbollah within the category of "Islamofascism."

3. In an interview published in the Beirut daily *L'OrientLe Jour* on March 1, 2004, Elias Atallah – a former leading member of the Lebanese Communist Party who led the National Front of the Lebanese Resistance (NFLR) until 1987, before he split from the party a few years later and joined the March 14 coalition – reported as follows: "We had to suffer in order to execute our resistance actions because of the 'privatization' of the security of the regions (each one controlled by a militia). This is the first time a people has to suffer 'from within' in order to be able to liberate its territory, in order to reach the occupation forces. NFLR members had to suffer in order to reach the 'security belt.' They were aggressed every day by the forces that controlled these regions."

4. The proclamation used the Arabic-Persian Khomeinist *mustazafeen* instead of the Arabic *mahrumeen* ("deprived") that Musa al-Sadr had used to designate his movement.

5. Thus, there is no civil code for personal status in Lebanon, but only the implementation of the rules pertaining to each religious denomination with regard to issues like marriage, inheritance, and so on.

6. Waddah Charara, *Dawlat "hizbullâh": lubnân mujtama'an islâmiyyan* (*"Hezbollah"'s State: Lebanon as an Islamic Society*) (Beirut: Dar al-Nahar, 1996). Charara's book, though thought-provoking, is affected by the author's extreme hostility toward his topic and his eagerness to

apply at all costs the "totalitarian" paradigm to the Shiite organization.

7. The same arrogance accounts for the frequency with which Washington reproaches Cuba and Venezuela for their interference in the affairs of other Latin American countries.

8. This area, comprising a few tens of square kilometers of Lebanese territory, was seized by Israel when it invaded the Syrian Golan Heights in 1967.

9. This was the explanation given by Naim Qassem, Hezbollah's deputy general secretary, in an interview (in Arabic) posted on Islamonline.net on October 25, 2005.

10. Walid Charara, "Ask Those Who Are Chiefly Concerned," (in Arabic), *al-Akhbar*, August 19, 2006. Walid Charara is the op-ed editor of this new daily and coauthor, with Frédéric Domont, of a book on Hezbollah: *Le Hezbollah: Un mouvement islamo-nationaliste* (Paris: Fayard, 2004). An expert on the subject, he has been exposed by his excessive indulgence toward the Shiite party to a reproach symmetrical to that expressed above (see Note 6) with regard to his namesake. Walid Charara tends to paint Hezbollah "red," whereas Waddah Charara paints it "brown" – abusively in both cases.

11. This last cause is all the more useful politically given that the dean of the detainees, Samir Kuntar, is of Druze descent. Nowadays the most prominent representative of a "Druze" Arab nationalist attitude, he continues to uphold what used to be the community's majority attitude as expressed by the originally feudal leadership of Kamal Jumblatt, followed by his son Walid. The latter eventually turned against Syria, Iran, and Hezbollah, aligning himself behind the Hariris and their Saudi and U.S. sponsors.

12. Transcript (in Arabic) posted on the website of the Islamic Resistance (moqawama.org).

13. Transcript (in Arabic) published in the Beirut daily *as-Safir* on August 28, 2006.

14. In particular, see Seymour Hersch's investigation, "Watching Lebanon," *New Yorker,* August 21, 2006, as well as Matthew Kalman, "Israel Set War Plan More Than a Year Ago," *San Francisco Chronicle,* July 21, 2006.

15. Stephen Farrell, "*The Times* Interview with Ehud Olmert: Full Transcript," *The Times* (London), August 2, 2006.

16. Gidi Weitz, "To Beirut If Necessary," *Haaretz,* August 11, 2006.

17. Steven Erlanger, "War Gives Israeli Leader Political Capital," *New York Times,* July 16, 2006.

Notes to Chapter 3

1. For details, see Chapter 4.

2. Efraim Inbar, "Prepare for the Next Round," *Jerusalem Post,* August 15, 2006.

3. Moshe Arens, "Let the Devil Take Tomorrow," *Haaretz,* August 13, 2006.

4. Both the United States and France concluded major arms deals with the Saudis during the Lebanon war in July 2006. On French interests, see Note 8 in Chapter 1.

5. Associated Press, "Draft U.N. Resolution on War in Lebanon," August 5, 2006.

6. Interview with *Le Monde,* July 27, 2006. Later on, the French press mentioned the reluctance of the French military brass to engage in what seems to them a very tricky situation – one that is all the more intimidating given that Hezbollah has just displayed its capacity to resist an offensive incomparably vaster than all the means that Paris and its European partners could line up on the ground, in Lebanon.

7. This calculation was made by a spokesperson of the Lebanese army who expressed his surprise about it, as reported in *Le Monde,* September 15, 2006.

8. In this connection, note that the International Security

Assistance Force (ISAF) is essentially a NATO force acting in Afghanistan as an auxiliary of U.S. troops under a mandate voted by the UN Security Council in December 2001.

9. Between May 8 and May 25, 2006, Italy organized in Sardinia a multinational air military exercise known as "Spring Flag 2006," with participation from several European aviations (Belgium, France, Germany, Netherlands, and the United Kingdom) as well as from the U.S. Air Force in Europe (USAFE). Rome invited the Israeli aviation to join (five F-15I "Ra'am" took part in the exercise), prompting the withdrawal of Sweden, which initially was supposed to be involved in the scheme. The Israeli aviation had already participated in joint exercises with the German and Italian aviations.

10. Transcript (in Arabic) published in the daily *as-Safir* (Beirut), August 13, 2006; emphasis added.

11. Nasrallah returned to a triumphalist discourse in the big mass rally celebrating his organization's "divine victory" on September 22, 2006. The expression "divine victory" (*nasr ilâhi*) draws on Hezbollah's religious ideology as well as on the personality cult organized around its leader. (In Arabic, Nasrallah's name means "God's victory").

12. Arens, "Let the Devil Take Tomorrow."

13. Of all the countries taking part in the new UNIFIL, France is the only one that has an aircraft-carrier, a fact that makes its role indispensable in the context of clashes on the ground. Italy and Spain each have a much smaller aircraft-carrier. In October 2006, Paris was trying to obtain a UN mandate for sending its aircraft-carrier under the pretext of monitoring the Lebanese airspace so that the Israeli air force does not monitor it itself and thereby violate Lebanese sovereignty, giving Hezbollah further arguments for sticking to its armament.

14. Ze'ev Schiff, "Delayed Ground Offensive Clashes with Diplomatic Timetable," *Haaretz,* August 13, 2006.

15. A study published by the very pro-Israeli Washington Institute for Near East Policy, one month after the cease-fire in Lebanon, underlined with dismay "the slow pace of government reconstruction efforts – particularly when compared to the swift and comprehensive rehabilitation program currently being implemented by Iranian-backed Hizballah. Indeed, in addition to the $12,000 Hizballah has already provided to each of 5,000 homeless families, press accounts indicate that Hizballah has nearly completed its own damage survey of the Beirut suburbs … In addition to serving Shiite areas, Hizballah is also working in predominately Sunni areas, like the northern area of Akkar, where the Shiite militia reportedly recently repaired some two-hundred houses in thirteen villages." (See David Schenker, "Reconstructing Lebanon: Short and Longer Term Challenges," Policy Watch 1146, Washington Institute for Near East Policy, September 12, 2006.)

16. This proportion was more than 17 percent in 1996.

17. See Chapter 2.

18. See Chapter 1.

19. Again, see Chapter 1.

Notes to Chapter 4

1. Tanya Reinhart, "Israel's 'New Middle East,'" ZNet, July 26, 2006.

2. Yoel Marcus, "5 Comments on the Situation," *Haaretz,* August 29, 2006.

3. Charles Krauthammer, "Israel's Lost Moment," *Washington Post,* August 4, 2006.

4. "Address by Foreign Minister Ehud Barak to the Annual Plenary Session of the National Jewish Community Relations Advisory Council, February 11, 1996," MFA Library, Ministry of Foreign Affairs website (www.mfa.gov. il).

5. Ralph Peters, "Can Israel Win?" *New York Post,* July 22, 2006.

6. Gidi Weitz, "To Beirut If Necessary," *Haaretz,* August 11, 2006.

7. Uri Avnery, "What the Hell Has Happened to the Army?" August 12, 2006, Gush Shalom website (gushshalom. org).

8. Daniel Ben Simon, "Betrayed by the State," *Haaretz,* September 4, 2006.

9. Uzi Benziman, "Pulling the Wool over Our Eyes," *Haaretz,* August 30, 2006.

10. Uzi Benziman, "Who's in the Bunker?" *Haaretz,* September 3, 2006.

11. Avraham Tal, "Preparing for the Next War Now," *Haaretz,* August 17, 2006.

12. Ze'ev Schiff, "We Need a Strategic Revolution," *Haaretz,* September 1, 2006.

13. Ronnie Kasrils, "Rage of the Elephant: Israel in Lebanon," *Mail & Guardian,* Johannesburg, September 1, 2006.

Notes to Conclusion

1. Charles Krauthammer, "Israel's Lost Moment," *Washington Post,* August 4, 2006.

2. Thomas Friedman, "Time for Plan B," *New York Times,* August 4, 2006.

3. Charles Krauthammer, "The Unipolar Moment," in G. Allison and G. F. Treverton, eds., *Rethinking America's Security: Beyond Cold War to New World Order* (New York: W. Norton, 1992), pp. 295–306.

4. Mike Allen and Romesh Ratnesar, "The End of Cowboy Diplomacy," *Time,* July 17, 2006.

5. Stefan Halper and Jonathan Clarke, "Twilight of the Neocons," *Washington Monthly,* March 2004.

6. Edward Luttwak, "A Post-Heroic Military Policy,"

Foreign Affairs, vol. 75, no. 4 (July/August 1996).

7. For a description of this process, see Noam Chomsky and Gilbert Achcar, *Perilous Power: The Middle East and U.S. Foreign Policy* (Boulder, Colo.: Paradigm Publishers, 2007).

8. Ze'ev Sternhell, "The Most Unsuccessful War," *Haaretz,* August 2, 2006.

9. Saad Eddine Ibrahim, "The 'New Middle East' Bush Is Resisting," *Washington Post,* August 23, 2006. The survey is described on the Institute's website (www.eicds.org).

Index

Sub-headings are arranged in ascending page order.